Women of Horror and Speculative Fiction in Their Own Words

Women of Horror and Speculative Fiction in Their Own Words

Conversations with Authors, Editors, and Publishers

Edited by
SÉBASTIEN DOUBINSKY
and CHRISTINA KKONA

BLOOMSBURY ACADEMIC
NEW YORK · LONDON · OXFORD · NEW DELHI · SYDNEY

BLOOMSBURY ACADEMIC
Bloomsbury Publishing Inc
1385 Broadway, New York, NY 10018, USA
50 Bedford Square, London, WC1B 3DP, UK
29 Earlsfort Terrace, Dublin 2, Ireland

BLOOMSBURY, BLOOMSBURY ACADEMIC and the Diana logo are trademarks of
Bloomsbury Publishing Plc

First published in the United States of America 2024

Cover design by Gita Kowlessur and Eleanor Rose
Cover image © Gita Kowlessur

Bloomsbury Publishing Inc does not have any control over, or responsibility for,
any third-party websites referred to or in this book. All internet addresses given
in this book were correct at the time of going to press. The author and publisher
regret any inconvenience caused if addresses have changed or sites have
ceased to exist, but can accept no responsibility for any such changes.

Library of Congress Cataloging-in-Publication Data

Names: Doubinsky, Sébastien, 1963- editor. | Kkona, Christina, editor.
Title: Women of horror and speculative fiction in their own words : conversations with
authors and editors / edited by Sébastien Doubinsky and Christina Kkona.
Description: New York : Bloomsbury Academic, 2024. | Includes index. | Summary: "The first
work to bring together women authors and editors of science fiction, horror and fantasy to
speak about their experiences, providing a unique glimpse into how gender and genre are
linked in these literary categories"– Provided by publisher.
Identifiers: LCCN 2023028900 (print) | LCCN 2023028901 (ebook) |
ISBN 9781501384462 (hardcover) | ISBN 9781501384455 (paperback) |
ISBN 9781501384479 (e-pub) | ISBN 9781501384486 (pdf) |
ISBN 9781501384493 (e-book)
Subjects: LCSH: Women authors–Interviews. | Horror tales–Women authors–History
and criticism. | Speculative fiction–Women authors–History and criticism. |
Science fiction–Women authors–History and criticism. | Fantasy fiction–
Women authors–History and criticism. | Women and literature. |
Feminism in literature. | LCGFT: Literary criticism. | Interviews.
Classification: LCC PN471 .W636 2024 (print) | LCC PN471 (ebook) |
DDC 809/.9164082—dc23/eng/20230928
LC record available at https://lccn.loc.gov/2023028900
LC ebook record available at https://lccn.loc.gov/2023028901

ISBN: HB: 978-1-5013-8446-2
            PB: 978-1-5013-8445-5
            ePDF: 978-1-5013-8448-6
            eBook: 978-1-5013-8447-9

Typeset by RefineCatch Limited, Bungay, Suffolk
Printed and bound in Great Britain

To find out more about our authors and books visit www.bloomsbury.com
and sign up for our newsletters.

CONTENTS

ACKNOWLEDGMENTS

AIAS (Aarhus Institute of Advanced Studies)

Marie Skłodowska-Curie Actions

Introduction

Equally indefinable, the concepts of "genre" and "gender" separately or in their intertwinements have triggered and continue to trigger innumerable debates. The defining process becomes even more complex, if we acknowledge the intersectional character of both gender and genre, and their multiple understandings in the different places, cultural spaces, racial affinities, social classes, and temporalities that compose the world in its current state.

This anthology of conversations with writers and editors who identify as women in the Western post-identitarian moment offers to its readers the opportunity to discover contemporary women of different national, racial, social, and sexual backgrounds who either publish or write in the genres of speculative fiction and horror including the various subgenres of these major categories.

Women and Genre Fiction

If Madame Bovary exemplifies the image of the female reader of mass culture in the nineteenth century, *Orlando* is to the eyes of its author "all a joke; and yet gay and quick reading I think; a writer's holiday."[1] Female readers are more easily lured to mass culture, while renowned female writers need to dismiss their experiments with genre fiction as parerga. To break away from high modernist

---

[1] Woolf, Virginia. Diary, vol. 3, March 18, 1928, 177.

production, Virginia Woolf somehow turns to the literature of consumption. With the exception of the *New York Times* that praised its groundbreaking qualities,[2] *Orlando* was mostly regarded as a gossip novel around the works and days of Vita Sackville-West rather than a masterpiece and became an immediate financial success. *Orlando*'s lack of realism and its belonging to multiple genres (biography, history, fantasy, and romance)[3] blocked its gateway to the realm of high art. From the end of the nineteenth century until recently, gothics, mysteries, romances, science fiction, horror, and all other kinds of nonrealistic fiction were considered as "subliterary genres of mass culture," as Frederic Jameson termed them as late as 1981.[4]

These preconceptions foreshadow or reflect what has been known as the "Great Divide," articulated in different though similar terms by its first theoreticians. In his *Theory of the Novel*, Lukács separates the Novel from its evil twin the entertainment novel; Greenberg establishes a distinction between avant-garde literature and kitsch, while Adorno and Horkheimer talk about serious versus light art. Certainly, this divide attributed to an underlying social or economic divide could explain the educational gap between middle and upper class and the working classes. In the late nineteenth and early twentieth centuries, at the moment when English Literature was first established as an academic subject, white male individuals of the upper classes were the only ones to receive university education. Independently from their political affiliations and their esthetic differences, the aforementioned literary theorists along with their British counterparts, the Modernist critics who were at the same time the first generation of English Literature scholars, deplored the decline of culture. According to them, it radicalized the divide between a higher, rigorous, and more demanding art that criticizes dominant structures, on the one hand, and, on the other, the "cultural industry" or the easily digestible mass culture that offers entertainment and serves to spread propaganda. Aesthetic

---

[2]https://archive.nytimes.com/www.nytimes.com/books/97/06/08/reviews/woolf-orlando.html

[3]English, Elizabeth. *Lesbian Modernism: Censorship, Sexuality and Genre Fiction.* Edinburgh University Press, 2017, 16.

[4]Jameson, Fredric. *Political Unconscious: Narrative as a Socially Symbolic Act.* Cornell University Press, 1982.

originality and stylistic experimentation are here aligned with politics of resistance while the mainstream, market-driven, and formulaic fictional production becomes a tool for manipulation.

In his seminal albeit controversial *After the Great Divide*, Andreas Huyssen discusses the gendering of mass culture/modernism dichotomy that assimilates mass culture to women. "The powerful masculinist and misogynist current within the trajectory of modernism"[5] womanized the masses, as "the male fear of woman and the bourgeois fear of the masses becomes indistinguishable."[6] Women and their liberation movements, sexuality and the unconscious, the dismantlement of the hegemonic subject are targeted by the phallocentric bourgeoisie. The othering of popular literature becomes an indirect way of segregating the other gender or class. Beyond any other reason, it is also this historical connection between genre and gender that triggered the inception of this anthology.

In a famous statement, Huyssen declares: "Modernism constituted itself through a *conscious strategy of exclusion*, an anxiety of contamination by its *other*: an increasingly engulfing mass culture."[7] The binarism of this statement has been criticized and rebuked by other historians of modernism who do not see a radical opposition between applauded and marginalized literature, but rather aspire to the reevaluation of both pleasurable canonical texts and "artistic" literary entertainment.[8] Nonetheless, the split between valuable cultural products and their commercial counterparts persists today at least for academics, despite the changes in institutionalized cultural appreciation and in the universities' and literary departments' structure and curricula.

Popular novels, bestsellers, pulp fiction, and other similar expressions described the literary other, what was not Literature for the academic circles, until the 1970s when the term "genre fiction"

[5]Huyssen, Andreas. *After the Great Divide: Modernism, Mass Culture, Postmodernism*. Indiana University Press, 1986, 49.
[6]Ibid., 52.
[7]Ibid., vii.
[8]Scholes, Robert E. "Exploring the Great Divide: High and Low, Left and Right." *Narrative* 11, no. 3 (2003): 256.

in its current sense—as opposed to literary fiction—first emerged.[9] Up to that moment, these uncategorized novels were grouped according to their commercial worth rather than their stylistic or generic specificities. The term "genre" attributed a certain status and visibility to the great variety of marginalized novels both conceived by and destined to an audience that did not belong to the elite of literary departments. Therefore, the academic understanding of genre as a literary categorization from Aristotle to Northrop Frye and beyond has not much to share with the glossary of genre fiction that mainly served library shelving, publishing series, and marketing promotion.

Conventionally excluded from the realm of literature and its subgenres, genre fiction is meant to replicate formulaic patterns and conventions that as such preclude structural innovations, stylistic refinement, and introspective thought. But genre fiction, like all fiction, is noticeable once it challenges boundaries, in this case generic conventions, in order to restructure or redefine the category to which it belongs. "Genre fiction," not unlike "literary genre," is a dynamic term, and shares the same power and limits. It is worth noting that the expression "genre fiction" is originally specific to the English language and only sometimes borrowed/transposed in Spanish or Italian, but generally still not used in French where "paralittérature" is the most common term. In German, it is simply copied as "Genre Fiktion." This is revealing about the globalization of marketing strategies, even when the lexemes "gender" and "genre" are expressed by completely different (German) or, conversely, identical signifiers (French, Spanish). It is not only subject to space and time, but redefines itself every time it becomes more inclusive: it has been transformed by women's writing, postcolonial additions, and sexual minorities' contributions. But as there is no coherence in history or clear-cut oppositions, there are moments when the marginalized, even when considered conservative as in the case of pulp fiction, assume their revolutionary power. Censorship of obscene literature in early-twentieth-century Britain banned *The Well of Loneliness* but spared *Orlando*, "because the

---

[9]Gupta, Suman Das. "On Mapping Genre: Literary Fiction/Genre Fiction and Globalization Processes." In Jernej Habjan and Fabienne Imlinger, eds., *Globalizing Literary Genres: Literature, History, Modernity.* Routledge, 2016, 213–27.

experimental text navigated censorship by strategically encoding sexual material."[10] Against Woolf's own fears, the novel has been "canonized" due to its elusiveness. At the same time, "genre fiction" judged too trivial to be considered as a national threat became a safe haven for the sexually or nationally other. As Elisabeth English points out, "at a time of intense censorship, genre fiction served as a strategy for writing the lesbian and provided a language for modernist and mainstream authors alike to navigate and make sense of the social and cultural complexities of the time."[11]

Speculative Fiction, Horror, and Gender

Speculative fiction is by definition haunted by the *other*: aliens, ghosts, cyborgs, monsters, and other hybrid and supernatural creatures populate its different universes. Since the early period of pulp science fiction, the *other* tormented the exclusively straight, white, middle-class male creators, readers, and protagonists of these stories. The genre was somehow preordained to attract female writers, who pursued their activities in the dark. Mary Shelley's and Charlotte Perkins Gilman's legacies seem to have influenced many invisible women writers and publishers prior to the New Wave of the 1960s, when they—at least white, middle-class straight women—gained greater visibility both as writers and strong fictional characters. The influence of postmodernism and surrealism over the stylistic and thematic experimentations of the 60s along with the ramifications of the sexual liberation movement and the enhanced use of the Social Sciences as opposed to the masculinist hardcore science marked a significant turn in the evolution of the genre by introducing new themes, reframing its conventions, challenging Western premises about imperialism and technological progress as well as social norms related to sex, race, and gender.[12] Meanwhile, the works of writers such as Ursula K. Le Guin, Joanna Russ, James Tiptree, Jr., and many others demonstrated the

---

[10]English, 8.

[11]Ibid., 2.

[12]For a detailed historical overview of the genres of science fiction and fantasy, see Reid, Robin Anne, dir. *Women in Science Fiction and Fantasy*. Greenwood Press, 2008.

importance of feminist thought since the 1960s and paved the way for the feminist science fiction of the 70s.

Feminist science fiction did not content itself with reforming the masculinist pulp science fiction conventions but immersed itself in questioning social inequality, rethinking power relations, and challenging gender stereotypes through imagining alternative settings. Le Guin has the merit of having popularized the gender-informed science fiction novel with *The Left Hand of Darkness* (1969). But feminism did not only tackle gender stereotypes, but unearthed questions of sexuality, race, class, and species. Russ was one of the first science fiction writers to thematize lesbianism; Octavia Butler was the first acclaimed African-American science fiction writer with a visibly intersectional work, while Marge Piercy in her *Woman on the Edge of Time* (1976) dared to create a Chicana protagonist.

During the second-wave feminism of the 1970s, Ellen Moers's coinage of the term "female gothic" marked a pivotal moment in the understanding of the centrality of gender in the gothic—horror literature's most distilled expression. Along with Moers's effort to recover the lost tradition of women's literature, the 70s saw the advent of exemplary works such as Jean Rhys's *Wide Sargasso Sea* (1966), arguably the first contemporary, postcolonial women's gothic fiction and Angela Carter's *The Magic Toyshop* (1967). Both novels revisit successfully gothic tropes, "while also exposing the silencing and disempowerment of women under colonialism and imperialism, and in Carter's case, the entrapping gendered narratives of fairytale and myth".[13] The genre's evolution in terms of the representation of the feminine was very much indebted to Daphne du Maurier's work and her reconfiguration of gothic romance in *Rebecca* (1938) and to Shirley Jackson's retelling of the haunted house story in *The Haunting of Hill House* (1959).

The success of fantasy and horror genres impelled mainstream literary writers of the 1980s such as Angela Carter, Margaret Atwood, and Doris Lessing to introduce science fiction and horror elements in their work. At the same time, writers such as Le Guin

---

[13]Wisker, Gina. *Contemporary Women's Gothic Fiction: Carnival, Hauntings and Vampire Kisses*. Palgrave Macmillan, (12) 2016.

and Piercy were adopted into the mainstream literary world. The 80s saw, among others, the emergence—or, rather, the popularization—of cyberpunk with Pat Cadigan (*Mindplayer*, 1987) and Melissa Scott being among its most prominent female representatives. 80s science fiction marks the passage from woman to women. Donna Haraway's "A Cyborg Manifesto: Science, Technology and Socialist-Feminism in the Late Twentieth Century" tackles the universal, totalizing ambitions of both Marxist and radical feminist theories.[14] Revealing the feminist shortcomings in terms of understanding the experiential specificities on the level of race, class, and sexuality, Haraway analyzes the inherent fragmentation of both individual and communities and the irrelevance of the concept of identity itself.[15, 16]

On the level of gothic horror, women writers embrace, refute, or satirize the construction of women as abject. Angela Carter, Margaret Atwood, and Nalo Hopkinson ("The Glass Bottle Trick," 2000) opt for the rewriting of myths, while Toni Morrison and Sarah Waters (*Fingersmith*, 2012) bring to the fore silenced, mistreated, and marginalized women. Some more radical writers, such as Jewelle Gomez (*The Gilda Stories*, 1991) and Elfriede Jelinek (*Illness or Modern Women*, 1987), celebrate abjection transforming the other into an agent of radical energy.

As we have seen, genre fiction has been relegated to the "literature of escape, and not of expression,"[17] and as such it can evade questions of race, class, and gender. However, the growing diversity of writers as well as their engagement with current challenges have indeed demonstrated the potential of the genre in imagining alternative power structures beyond gender and race binaries and

---

[14]*Simians, Cyborgs and Women: The Reinvention of Nature*. Free Association Books, 1991.
[15]She argues that "the cyborgs populating feminist science fiction make very problematic the statuses of man or woman, human, artifact, member of a race, individual entity, or body".
[16]In other words, they challenge the persistent dualism of Western traditions in innovative ways. Discussing Vonda N. McIntyre's *Superluminal*, she claims that the novel "embodies textually the intersection of feminist theory and colonial discourse".
[17]English, 12.

sexual behaviors beyond heteronormative desires. Imagining humans as aliens enabled the inception of Ursula Le Guin's alternative gender identities and Octavia Butler's hybridized bodies that move and act in alternative realms. Somehow these works fictionalized the plasticity, multiplicity, and malleability of the post-identitarian subject.

Since the 1990s, the proliferation of speculative fiction novels and the increasing presence of online publications contributed to the greater visibility of women readers, writers, and editors and to the emergence of marginalized voices. However, the unraveling of the density and multiplicity underpinning the women's speculative fiction and horror works of the last thirty years is yet to be satisfactorily done. Our *Conversations* aim to fill some of these critical gaps.

The Genre of the Interview

This book is an anthology of *Conversations*. The word "conversation" may seem either irrelevant or a euphemism, given that Covid-19 restrictions and the subsequent cancelation of conventions allowed us only to conduct email interviews and, if we dare say, literary interviews. However, we can call them conversations, as long as the interviewers are not journalists but scholars and readers of the work of these writers and publishers. In addition, for Seb Doubinsky, a writer of speculative fiction himself, the interviewees are friends and colleagues.

Interviews are currently ubiquitous in all journalistic media: print, audiovisual, digital, or multimedia. For a writer or a publisher, as for every public figure or private individual, the interview is a means of visibility that can contribute to one's celebrity or serve as a marketing device. For readers, the interview is meant to be a simple and straightforward access to a writer's work, personality, ideas, or positions. However, our anthology does not consist of interviews of general interest; it has a thematic format structured around the relationship between genre and gender and therefore the interviewees are invited to respond to a partially personalized questionnaire. Thus, it is guided by our line of thought and the need to bring to light an up-to-date overview of the current challenges of female genre fiction publishers and writers. The publication of these interviews in the form of a book presupposes that we value them as independent texts, edited as little as possible in order to reflect the personal take of each participant, that are meant to serve as sources for research on literary works and authors.

We usually talk about "literary interview" when a literary person is involved in the process, either as interviewer or interviewee and most commonly when the interviewee is a creative writer, without necessarily implying that it is a subgenre of the personal interview or that it holds any literary value. The literary interview, more or less in its current form, emerged to complement the predominance or the professionalization of criticism after the Second World War. Against what New Criticism identified as intentional fallacy, a series of literary reviews—if we were to exclude the interviews in the media of general interest—starting with the *Paris Review* in 1953[18] attempted to promote the professional autonomy of writers beyond criticism. Long out of critical scope, the interview gained recently much attention under the lead of scholars such as Anneleen Masschelein, Rebecca Roach, and Galia Yanoshevsky, who have initiated what has been called "Interview Studies."[19] Roach's *Literature and the Rise of the Interview* and Yanoshevsky's *L'Entretien littéraire. Anatomie d'un genre* filled the gap of the historical and genetic approach to the interview in both American and European traditions. To our knowledge, there has not been any comprehensive study of the literary interview in the rest of the world.

According to Gerard Genette's classification, the interview can be considered as a paratext,[20] rather than as a genuine literary text in its own right, while for Philippe Lejeune it is a modern form of autobiographical practice.[21] There is no consensus with regard to the generic form of the interview even in most recent critical approaches. In a long and instructive article, Masschelein et al.

---

[18]Williams, Jeffrey J. "The Rise of the Critical Interview." *New Literary History* 50, no. 1 (2019): 4.

[19]Williams, Jeffrey J. "Literature and the Rise of the Interview by Rebecca Roach." *Biography* 42, no. 4 (2019): 929.

[20]Genette, Gérard. *Paratexts: Thresholds of Interpretation.* Cambridge University Press, 1997.

[21]Philippe, Lejeune. *Je est un autre : L'autobiographie de la littérature aux médias.* Seuil, 1980.

theorize the interview as a hybrid genre.[22] As Masschelein et al. suggest, "its functional closeness to (and rivalry with) existing," mainly nonfictional, genres as well as to literary currents in certain periods, and, finally, its recourse to narrative and stylistic devices are widely seen as literary. None of these criteria is a sufficient marker of literary generic status; we would rather see them as "preconditions" for becoming a genre. Secondly, the interview is a two-step procedure that reflects two different types of discourse: the oral or written dialogue and the edited text. The conversation that as such is marked by spontaneity, improvisation, etc., cannot easily conform to a generic frame, usually linked to an authorial function contrary to the edited text that is the result of collaboration between interviewer and interviewee. The antagonism between interviewer and interviewee that may occur in different contexts has no place in this volume. The different chapters correspond to the different interviews that we have received in written form and there has been no need either for transcription or metacommentaries, except for the introduction and the biographical notes. Therefore, the editors of this volume do not make any claims to authorship, if we make abstraction of the questionnaires and the overall structuring of the book. As a result of a dialogical though asymmetrical relation, these conversations lead to different kinds of texts, more or less literary, detailed, autobiographical, etc., depending on the interviewee, who is the one to decide how to set boundaries between private and public, secrecy and revelation. The volume is structured with the ultimate respect for the different styles, ideas, and choices of the interviewees. They are writers in practice even though this practice is not meant to be fictional. Nevertheless, they are free to invent the self or persona who responds to our questions not unlike an autobiographical text or the creation of their fictional characters. Certainly, these interviews have been conducted on the basis of some shared principles: the honesty and truthfulness of the responses is part of the expectations from an interview with a writer or a publisher. It is also the reader's usual wishful thinking that one's work reflects one's life. It's up to the interviewee to decide the degree to which her responses are in consistency with her fictional

---

[22]Masschelein, A., C. Meuree, D. Martens, and S. Vanasten. "The Literary Interview: Toward a Poetics of a Hybrid Genre." *Poetics Today* nos. 35, 1–2 (2014): 1–49.

universe or with her experience in the case of discrepancies between her narratives or personas. As a hybrid genre, the literary interview can transgress the boundaries between fact and fiction and it is not up to the interviewers to pronounce a verdict.

A Note on Our Interaction with the Interviewees

In what follows, we question editors and writers on general assumptions, stereotypical views, and prejudices around the female presence in speculative fiction and its currents. The questions do not necessarily reflect our preconceptions about literary, generic, or gender issues, but constitute an effort to bring different reading communities closer. The various actors of the current speculative fiction landscape respond to some issues we have touched on in this Introduction such as gender discrimination and challenges, gender visibility, the gender/genre affinities in their lives and works, the representation/thematization of gender in their chosen genres, the aesthetic and political relevance of their choices. We have provided our guests with a standard questionnaire to which we have added some questions related to each person's published works. We wanted to emphasize intersectionality and inclusiveness and we were thrilled to observe that the responses went beyond our expectations by covering aspects that we had neglected in our questions such as the representation of disabilities and neurodiversity; the internet and social media impact on their visibility and work; the influence of film and tv series on the creation and reception of speculative genres.

We have tried our best to include in our volume women from as many nationalities and/or ethnicities as possible who have published in English or have been translated into it. Voices from different social, cultural, and educational backgrounds around the world give their insight on the current production in genre fiction and help us expand and/or update our definitions of notions such as genre, horror, danger, diversity, etc.

We welcomed the critique and manipulations of our questions and respected the silence of the interviewees whenever they decided not to respond. Sometimes they asked for clarification, but we did not comply, as we preferred to receive answers based on the interviewees' own understanding of our words.

We traveled all around the world and in alternative worlds with these female voices, their ideas, and their works while isolated by Covid-19 quarantines and immobilized behind our screens. They can certainly trigger even more improbable journeys.

CHAPTER ONE

Eugen Bacon

Eugen Bacon (born in 1971) is an award-winning African-Australian horror and speculative fiction writer. Notable works: *Claiming T-Mo* (novel, 2019), *Danged Black Things* (collection, 2020).

Thank you very much for accepting to discuss with us the intertwining between gender and genre with regard to your own work and to speculative fiction in its broader sense (science fiction, fantasy, horror, utopian, and dystopian fiction, etc.), to which you have recently dedicated a clear and thorough handbook: *Writing Speculative Fiction: Creative and Critical Approaches* (Red Globe Press, 2019).

Speculative fiction—and science fiction, in particular—has traditionally been regarded as a male-oriented genre. Before the advent of second-wave feminism and the gay liberation movement in the 1960s, women writers were denied recognition not as much by publishing houses as by science fiction nominations and awards. Even today, science fiction is considered as mainly appealing to men and fantasy as being more welcoming to women. How do you feel about this gender-oriented differentiation among genres?

Marion Zimmer Bradley answers this question in her prologue to *The Door Through Space* (1961):

> I discovered s-f in its golden age: the age of Kuttner, C. L. Moore, Leigh Brackett, Ed Hamilton and Jack Vance. But while I was still collecting rejection slips for my early efforts, the fashion changed. Adventures on faraway worlds and strange dimensions

went out of fashion, and the new look in science-fiction—
emphasis on the science—came in.

So my first stories were straight science-fiction, and I'm not
trying to put down that kind of story. It has its place. By and
large, the kind of science-fiction which makes tomorrow's
headlines as near as this morning's coffee has enlarged popular
awareness of the modern, miraculous world of science we live in.
It has helped generations of young people feel at ease with a
rapidly changing world.[1]

The times of emergence, and the history of *both* science fiction
and fantasy, determined who wrote it, without a necessary gender-
oriented differentiation *between* the two genres. Both were white
and male-dominated, comprising those stories published in a US
science fiction magazine or specialist press.

But hard science fiction, more than fantasy, became a subculture
of writers, editors, fans, and critics for its science and technological
slant. The New Wave era with its cultural speculation, soft sciences,
and psychology encouraged stories that were less science- or
technology-driven, which at the time belonged to a man's world,
paving the way for more white women writers. The times were not
right in Europe or the US for the black voice, with the history of
slavery and all that.

Fantasy, from the onset, welcomed the speculative aesthetics and
poetics that might attract the female writer whose curiosity is open
to fairy tales, magic, dragons, and the lush worlds that come along
with the fantastic. But it was still a man's world—the Brothers
Grimm, Hans Christian Andersen, Edgar Allan Poe, Philip K. Dick,
Arthur C. Clarke, Isaac Asimov . . . Think how difficult it was for
Mary Shelley to publish *Frankenstein* (1818).

It took a feminist breakthrough for writers such as Ursula Le
Guin to find a welcoming of their fantasy and science fiction novels
such as *The Dispossessed* (1974), a utopian novel that exemplifies
the effects of established colonies that subjugate others, and *The
Left Hand of Darkness* (1968), that takes place on an alien world
without sexual prejudice, where inhabitants of the planet could
shift between genders.

---

[1]Marion Zimmer Bradley, *The Door Through Space*. The Floating Press, 2011.

Did you encounter any discrimination specifically related to your gender in your writing career?
I think the discrimination I experienced as a writer was less to do with gender, and more to do with race. My writing kicked off in the UK and expanded in Australia, where I was submitting works to white publishers and white editors, and I didn't have the racial profile that the majority of readers identified with, or the 'right' networking to fast-track my career.

It took a PhD in creative writing for publishers and editors to notice, and now a paradigm shift where black speculative fiction is beginning to rise on the radar.

There is today an ongoing debate around the word "genre" in the science fiction/horror milieu. Some agree with Ursula K. Le Guin that it is socially prejudiced; others claim that it is an essential and necessary literary "identity." What is your position on the subject?
As a proponent of crossing genres, I think there's a problem with definitions. Labels are more to do with marketing than literary identity. A publisher will determine what genre your work fits. Genre boundaries remain thin, and it's mostly about where the work will sit on a bookshelf.

Bending genre is a sort of playfulness with language and form, a deviation from tradition, a blurring of boundaries that is fresh, invigorating. This is my position on the subject.

What is determinant in your choice of these genres?
What I write is literary speculative fiction—a hybrid that's perfect for the writer who is curious, exploratory, immersed in a creative space that is ever redefining itself. I've always loved literary writing, the poetics in language: metaphor, allusion, imagery, art as language. Marry this with speculative fiction and its "what if" quotient, and you get creative nirvana.

Literary speculative fiction enables a different kind of story that welcomes poeticity, diversity, possibility, fluency, association. One is not bound to the "rules" of genre. It invites the reader to approach it without demanding answers to the questions: *Is it science fiction? Or fantasy? Or horror?* What the reader gets is a story that explores a great big "what if," an unlimited boundary constrained only by imagination.

The 1960s and 70s are perhaps the most influential decades in the study of gender in speculative fiction. Not only was there an influx of female speculative fiction writers, but also many of these writers applied feminist theory to speculative fiction (Ursula K. Le Guin, Angela Carter, etc.). At the same time, the emergence of African-American female voices brought to light the intersectionality between gender and race. It is as if speculative fiction genres offered better than others the opportunity to challenge social conventions, especially gender, and to explore alternative sexualities and alliances. Is it the case in your work? Have you been influenced by specific writers of this generation?

Toni Morrison and Octavia Butler have strongly influenced my writing. Morrison, in her Nobel lecture, saw narrative as radical, "as creating us at the very moment it is being created." Hers was a space where language is infinite, where language begins before language. Butler wrote the kind of story that featured another like her. She heartened what is today black speculative fiction, its roots in Afrofuturism, stories that pay attention to the black protagonist.

Black speculative fiction focuses on black heroes, on black people stories, and casts a gaze on the complex and diverse experiences of African and Afro descendant peoples. Black speculative fiction is about black people taking ownership to reimagine a new Africa and her people, untarnished (or redefined) by colonialism.

What renders speculative fiction genres apt to engage in sexual politics?

Think of the writer as an agent of change. I guess speculative fiction (across the spectrum of science fiction, fantasy, and horror) offers a safe space to address in an infinite boundary those topics and themes that can be difficult to explore in the real world.

How are these genres modified in order to accommodate contemporary post-identitarian claims?

Speculative fiction is welcoming to dystopian and utopian fiction that includes stories of social justice or injustice. It accommodates novel ideas and ways to speak the unspeakable. Through possibilities, probabilities, and associations, speculative fiction explores the power of ideas and their profound importance to the individual, to the society. In black speculative fiction, black writers can reimagine new worlds, often where the balance of power is shifted.

In horror fiction, transgressive sexualities are meant to tame the uncanniness, to exorcize sexuality's threat to the self by weaving it into the trauma of horror. Did the enhancement of social acceptability recalibrate what startles, horrifies, or repulses either readers or characters?
Speculative fiction takes you to an immeasurable frontier where nothing is a limit. The same applies to horror fiction that can desensitize audiences from the macabre. It becomes problematic when that desensitization transcends into the everyday—for example, in copycat killers.
Perhaps it's a question of the chicken or the egg. Does horror fiction recalibrate society, or does social acceptability recalibrate what horrifies in fiction?

Did it address the need of structurally modifying the invention of alternative worlds?
I have no answer to this question. I hope it is not prescriptive, trying to shape or put a border around the creator's imaginary invention. How do you structurally modify creativity?

In "genre fiction" such as fantasy, speculative fiction, and other relatively formulaic genres, there seems to be a tension in character identity as well as plot structure and situations between recognizable stereotypes that characterize a genre and facilitate reading, on the one hand, and, on the other, the malleability of the imaginary allowed by the construction of alternative universes. How do you manage to negotiate this tension with respect to gender images?
I steer clear from stereotypes. My characters tell their own story in speculative fiction that bends genre. The stubbornness and experimental nature of my writing refuses tethering. So, I guess I've never really had to negotiate such tensions.

There has been a revival of speculative fiction genres in the 2010s, especially with the 2016 electoral victory of Donald Trump. The immediate success of the TV series *Handmaid's Tale*, based on Margaret Atwood's dystopian novel, is indicative. What is the function of speculative fiction literature under the Trump

administration, given that it destabilizes the settled and normative meanings of sex, gender, power, race, etc.?

I would shudder to imagine the Trump administration influencing any kind of literature other than sarcasm and parody. He's certainly given writers of humor much material from his words and actions.

Has this influenced your own writing and in what ways?
I have certainly written fictions with worthless leaders parodied from Trump. In one fiction, "The Water Runner" appearing in the AfroSF v4 anthology, there's a character named the Great Leader who owns the country's only Robotix company that controls everything. In dialogue between potential lovers, a woman's decision lies solely on her suitor's answer:

"She looked at him squarely and demanded, 'What's your position on the Great Leader?'

He nearly failed: 'I used to think he was a fockwit, but now . . .'

She swirled to leave. 'Clearly I was mistaken about you—'

But his palm hooked her elbow, and he cut her words with the right answer: 'Only a fool tests the deepness of a river with both feet.' Indeed, the Great Leader was nothing but a nincompoop. He'd already taken a sixteen-year-old as his fifth wife."

In another fiction that is microlit in a chapbook titled *It's Folking Political* (2020), there are cameos of a president:

"Obstruction
A breaking news alert
. . . dons a rainbow mask and livestream freedom of anonymity and projection. The mask locks in metaphors of emotions: angst and confusion, above all rage. Because it's rubbish to scramble behind locked windows, screening ideology from crows and ravens. What violation is there when arcades of chaos are full of extinct animals and fragments of spells that animate new creatures? Once upon a time quarantine meant something, until taboos went horribly wrong in local color, unseen clashes never aired after midnight. Posturing as criticism or the absence of story is the detritus of folklore inciting incidents in a presidential speech on stolen ground. Now we wait."

The several subcategories that emerged with regard to speculative fiction (gay, lesbian, transgender, feminist, black, Philippine), enhanced by the different anthologies that we can find in the market, not only signify the portrayal of specific identities or communities, but also each of them seems to address a specific audience. Do you write with a gendered audience in mind?

It's without concerted effort that I include diversity in my writing—in particular, black hero/ines, female empowerment, and sexual diversity in the cast.

Do you think that speculative fiction works are differently structured when addressed to traditionally under-portrayed individuals or communities?

I think all writing should be bold and brave in featuring, representing, and portraying the diversity of the real world. The speculative allows "extraordinary" storytelling in the literal sense of the word: odd, unexpected—which welcomes "othering." Speculative fiction, in its very nature, allows more potential to write the "other."

The risk is where those integral themes of social justice in weird and speculative fiction are abandoned as surreal fiction and never addressed in the relatable real world.

Is the portrayal of a minority specifically addressed to those that feel portrayed in these works?

Black speculative fiction heralds the black person and their story—in this manner, it is a type of fiction that works well to spotlight the other.

Examples of subgenres of black speculative fiction include cyberfunk (centered on transformative effects of computers, networks, and information technology); sword and soul (rooted in sorcery and the sword); blacktastic (fantastical adventures where black hero/ines find reward); steamfunk (based on nineteenth-century technology—e.g., with steam-powered guns and machines); dieselfunk (prioritizing elements of the Industrial Revolution—for example, the internal combustion engine); and Rococoa (alternate history—e.g., with a slavery or piracy backdrop).

Claiming T-Mo (Meerkat Press, 2019) is a hybrid novel—or what you would call "cross-genre"—about, among others, some hybrid characters (Myra, Vida, etc.). Parallel world and time travels (science fiction), the invention of a new language and magic (fantasy), the double (horror) coexist with genealogical mysteries, power abuse, and penitential colonies. Inventing a world of interspecies couplings and intergalactic migrations, you seem to unravel a very nuanced landscape of otherness that explores questions of immigration, racism, sexism, and fascism. Was this hybrid form necessary to the work's aesthetics and politics?

I approached writing *Claiming T-Mo*, this black speculative novel, with an understanding that my artistic formations are imprinted by external influences: family, self-experience, education, culture, society . . . The language I speak (and write) influences and exposes my preconditioning. As an African Australian, a cultural hybrid, I am the self and other. I am many.

Claiming T-Mo considers alterity arising from the relational founding of identity. When one parent is "nonhuman" and the other is fully human, the offspring (such as the characters Myra or Tempest) find themselves in a position of being inside and outside. They inhabit both worlds but are predominantly outside.

My black speculative novel embraces queer theory in its themes around the challenges and possibilities of being different, a breed of "others," and themes of welcoming "otherness."

With the exception of T-Mo/Odysseus, the story is narrated by women of different generations, as if you were following their evolution—not always linear—from child abuse to wonder women. It is as if these women were claiming T-Mo, as a masculine ideal, devoid of all patriarchal evil. Is women's struggle bound to oscillate between T-Mo and Odysseus?

Each female character (Silhouette, Salem, Myra, Tempest, Amber) in the story has a struggle that's individual—it is a finding of self, irrespective of T-Mo or Odysseus.

Do we need a female-hybrid figure to lead the fight against discrimination or exclusion?

If you consider countries like Germany, New Zealand, or Finland that are handling well the current coronavirus pandemic in the world today, you'll note they are led by women. This tells me what I already know as a woman. Female-hybrid or not, the world is a better place for the females in it.

CHAPTER TWO

Francesca Barbini

Francesca Barbini is an Italian-born writer, editor, and publisher who resides in Scotland. She founded her award-winning publishing company Luna Press Publishing in 2015.

Thank you very much for accepting to answer these few questions. This book is going to focus specifically on the notions of "gender" and "genre" as we believe that both are equally intersectional and are either confronted by or confronting territorial positions of dominance. In this light, can you tell us about your background and how this, in your eyes, influenced the person and publisher you are today?
I have been an avid reader of horror and fantasy, primarily, and science fiction to an extent, since I was a child. The Italian libraries and bookshops had a great selection of genre fiction (national or in translation) to keep me entertained for hours on end. Growing up I would pick books based on the ones whose title/cover/blurb scared me or intrigued me the most. The author was incidental to begin with, but you'd stick to one, if you enjoyed their stories. There was no internet, so no connection to an author's private life (you rarely knew what they looked like unless their face was on the back of the cover), and no review sites except for your friend who would recommend a novel based on how much blood had been spilled in the shortest amount of time, and whatever other family members were reading at the time.

Looking through these old books and comics when I go back to Italy, I would say that *most* of them are in fact written by men, but it's only something that I noticed as an adult, through life experience (not just through "publisher's life" experience). Naturally, traveling around the world and meeting new people, I was able to embrace the amazing variety that is all around us, and my library is richer for it.

Not once in my life as a genre reader in Italy was I ever told or made to feel by society at large that this type of fiction was not good, not for women, or not worth it: it was just there, for those interested in it. I have carried my passion for genre throughout the years, with a shift in what I favor.

I run a small press, which reflects me, as an individual, and my experiences. I focus on genre because I still love it. I am free of the constraints that bind traditional publishing and can choose who and what to publish. I have lived my life enjoying the world and its different cultures, and I am proud to represent authors from all over, who write in different languages and from different perspectives.

Speculative fiction—and science fiction, in particular—has traditionally been regarded as a male-oriented genre. Before the advent of second-wave feminism and the gay liberation movement in the 1960s, women writers were denied recognition not as much by publishing houses as by science fiction nominations and awards. Some women, such as Alice Bradley Sheldon, even used male pseudonyms in order to get published. How do you feel about this gender-oriented differentiation among genres? Do you feel it still exists?

Social media can be a very useful research tool. If you focus on genre groups you will still find voices who support the view that there's no such thing as a female speculative writer. I know several female authors who use their initials only, or a pseudonym, to avoid encountering these biases. But the countermovement, from the 1960s onwards, has had an impact, thanks in no small part to the presence of the web. I can't tell you how long it will take for this gender-oriented differentiation to completely disappear, but it's happening at all levels of publishing, in different measures.

Do you feel any gendered resistance in the milieu or in the reviews?
There is. Social media can often testify to that, and certain review sites will continue to support it, generally for economic reasons. It

affects retailers as well: I know of bookshops who would love to stock and sell certain books, but they don't because their clientele would simply stop coming to their shop.

Thankfully, you can choose to a large extent who you want to be surrounded by. Moreover, the UK genre community I experience is for the vast majority an inclusive one, proof that things are indeed changing for the better. But it takes everyone's effort to bring it about, from readers to publishers, to reviewers, to retailers.

Did you encounter any discrimination specifically related to your gender in your publishing career?
No. Or at least not that I know of.

There is today an ongoing debate around the word "genre" in the science fiction/horror milieu. Some agree with Ursula K. Le Guin that it is socially prejudiced; others claim that it is an essential and necessary literary "identity." What is your position on the subject? What has determined your choice of literature as a publisher?
It can be both.

The word "genre" functions like a symbol: it stands for a concept which people have come to associate with a specific literary genre, or category fiction: readers who are familiar with that genre will be attracted to books that fall under that category, and for that I find it useful. It's a signpost.

That said, I am completely against a conversation that sees a difference between "literary" and "genre" fiction, as if the former stood for "better writing," and the latter for a lesser example of fiction, with no meaning or artistic value.

Which leads me to the reasons why I publish science fiction and fantasy. I obviously have an innate attraction to genre fiction, as I mentioned earlier, and within this I have found some of the best examples of human expressions and writing styles.

Nobel Prize-winner Doris Lessing, in an interview for the *Boston Book Review*, famously said that "in science fiction is some of the best social fiction of our time." I couldn't agree more.

The 1960s and 70s are perhaps the most influential decades in the study of gender in speculative fiction and horror. Not only was there an influx of female writers, but also many of these writers applied feminist theory to speculative fiction (Ursula K. Le Guin, Angela

Carter, Shirley Jackson, etc.). At the same time, the emergence of African-American female voices brought to light the intersectionality between gender and race. It is as if speculative fiction and horror genres offered better than others the opportunity to challenge social conventions, especially gender, and to explore alternative sexualities and alliances. What, in your eyes, renders speculative fiction and horror genres apt to engage in sexual politics?
Many reasons.

Speculative fiction brings you the potential future, the alternative "now," the "what could be." An author can create what they'd wish to see in their lifetime, and bring it about by planting seeds of what things could be like. The hope perhaps is that if more people wrote about and read certain topics, it would normalize them and bring them into "reality" faster.

Another explanation can be found in the way speculative fiction and horror are seen as niche, with an experimental readership that would more likely be open to sexual politics.

Luna Press covers a variety of genres, from horror to speculative fiction and fantasy. Your authors also offer a very varied background, both gender-wise and culturally. Do you consciously try to mirror the diversity of identities in your publishing and in the choice of your authors, or do you see it just as a reflection of the evolution of the times?
A bit of both. As I mentioned earlier, my life has been enriched by the discovery of authors from different identities and cultures, so I am consciously on the lookout for diversity and for creating opportunities that lead to it. I want the whole world to know what amazing writers are out there and what science fiction and fantasy *tastes* like outside the anglophone world and outside the mainstream.

Equally, I believe that the existing conversation on inclusivity is encouraging a lot more authors to come forward, and I have noticed that in the submissions we receive: there is a lot more representation.

You publish both male and female writers. Do you feel there is a difference in writing between the genders? Are you sensitive to their narrative angles?
In their cover letter, for the most part, authors are happy to let you know how they identify, so from that point of view you

approach the story knowing the gender of the author and your natural biases kick in, in terms of your experience of gender and knowledge of the world, and perhaps you see certain narrative angles because of that. However, reading blind submissions is also very interesting, because once the bias has been removed, you'd be surprised at how many times you thought you knew and it's not the case.

As for being sensitive to narrative angles, you have to be. The discourse about gender or cultural appropriation, for example, has asked authors to become better writers and better human beings, making them question their choice of characters and plot to elevate their craft to something that can really speak to the readers, beyond expendable extras and cheap thrills.

Speculative fiction and horror have often represented situations of sexual, family, or political oppression, and many of the books you have published focus on these questions. As a publisher, are you specifically looking for these themes? Do you think genre literature has a specific "identity" that allows it to tackle these themes for a larger audience than mainstream literature?

Occasionally we set a focus subject for a particular submissions call, but generally we seem to receive stories that deal with these themes organically. Authors are always invited to become familiar with a publisher's catalog before submitting, so when they do, they see that we do deal with certain themes and feel that Luna Press is the right home for their stories. This, then, perpetuates itself to an extent.

I think genre literature is more daring on all fronts and lends itself to the exploration of these themes. This is also due to the presence of small and medium presses, who are able to take greater risks with authors and topics, than traditional publishers. Thanks to the internet, there is a lot more awareness of what is happening outside of the Big Four, and many people enjoy going down the less beaten track discovering new voices, as well as supporting small business rather than large corporations. The latest celebrity biography or fiction work (often written by someone other than said celebrity) may sell plenty, but it also leaves readers and writers disenamoured with the whole publishing industry. It makes people want to look for something "real" and "off-script" elsewhere.

Do you hope to make a difference with Luna Press when it comes to gender issues and narratives (whether cis or LGBT+)? If yes, in what way?
I hope so, both in our fiction and nonfiction. Writing about and exploring gender issues and narratives helps to normalize the discourse and can help bring about equality among genders. Also, let's not forget the *whole* discourse—for example, we shouldn't forget the importance of writing more diverse male characters, as that will also have a knock-on effect on bringing about equality.

Luna Press also has an academic side, consisting in thematic volumes with academic articles. Would you consider academic writing a genre in itself? And is choosing to combine the fields of literary creation with academic reflections a provocation or an attempt of conciliation?
Academia Lunare is the academic arm of speculative nonfiction of Luna Press: we publish monographs, proceedings, calls for papers, reference books, etc. I do consider nonfiction a genre in itself, and in my press' case, tied to speculative fiction.

To me, one of the most exciting aspects of fandom is the critical assessment of speculative literature, as a way to go beyond the book and ground it in a wider social context. Speculative nonfiction is thus a mirror for society.

Our calls for papers, in particular, are the result of cross-disciplinary collaboration, which I consider an asset, and the beginning of many more journeys.

Provoking new ideas, while at the same time conciliating speculative fiction and nonfiction, is precisely what we set out to do.

CHAPTER THREE

J. S. Breukelaar

J.S. Breukelaar is an award-winning American-born horror and speculative fiction writer currently living in Australia. Notable works: *Aletheia* (novel, 2017), *The Bridge* (novella, 2021).

Thank you very much for accepting to answer these few questions. This book is going to focus specifically on the notions of "gender" and "genre" as we believe that both are equally intersectional and are either confronted by or confronting territorial positions of dominance. In this light, can you tell us about your background and how this, in your eyes, influenced the person and the writer you are today?

My background has had a direct influence on my writing, not only the kinds of fiction I write, but my entire outlook as a writer and a person. I was raised in a remote college town in upstate New York in the 1970s, and I was deeply immersed, as children are, in the woodsy, ancient "apartness" of the town—the presence of native Senecans and Cayugans, which at that time, depending on which teacher you had, was either a romanticized "absence" or a troubling and intrusive call to action. I was fortunate in that I had a teacher who I believe may have had Native American heritage and who was very much of the latter view. She got her sixth graders to think about that, and to think about all kinds of other things. Gender, capitalism, conservation, compassion. She literally got me writing by introducing journaling to me, and I've been doing it ever since. The other aspect of my background that made me the writer that I am is being displaced here in Australia. My family relocated to

Sydney when I was a teenager, and it was a deeply traumatic experience in more ways than one. It's not that I'm not glad to be here now—but it took a long time for me to make peace with what I felt had been taken from me.

Alienation and displacement are constant themes in my writing, as are gender politics and genre crossing, and I have this kind of background to blame for this.

Speculative fiction—and science fiction, in particular—has traditionally been regarded as a male-oriented genre. Before the advent of second-wave feminism and the gay liberation movement in the 1960s, women writers were denied recognition not as much by publishing houses than by science fiction nominations and awards. Even today, science fiction is considered as mainly appealing to men and fantasy as being more welcoming to women. How do you feel about this distinction? Did you encounter any discrimination specifically related to your gender in your writing career?
Very few. I know I'm fortunate. I have spoken with parents of all genders who, like me, found themselves not in a financial position to write fiction when their children were small, so I don't necessarily think that being a mother, rather than a father, in my case at least affected that. My academic career is a different story. My personal experience and that of many of my female colleagues is that as a working mother trying to build a university career, you encounter hurdles that a father doesn't necessarily have. This is changing rapidly but I have been in several teaching teams where the women, for whatever reason, end up doing the brunt of the administration work, and are consequently left behind when it comes to promotions and grant bids based on a strong record of research and publications. But that could just be some of the universities I've experienced, and I like to believe that it isn't everywhere.

Do you think women in horror and science fiction are in a better position today than when you began to write? Do you feel any gendered resistance in the milieu or in the reviews?
Yes, although that might appear to contradict what I said earlier. While I didn't personally encounter any gendered resistance when I began to write, I think that the last ten years have seen a centralization of issues that stereotypically are associated with cis women, such as menstruation, pregnancy, childbearing and so on—an insistence on

their validity, a refusal to whisper about them, or to accept a gaze that diminishes, say, the experience of having your first period, or feeling maternal guilt, or prioritizing the domestic sphere over the political because as Mary Shelley and her mom insisted, the domestic sphere is always political.

I also think that to a large degree we have comedians and female performers to thank for this. It takes guts to stand up before hundreds or thousands of people and talk about vaginas in a world where men and their penises are the norm. Imagine *Portnoy's Complaint* written by a woman. Imagine if Diderot had instead been Dorothy rummaging away beneath the sheets! So I think it's great that we have women standing up and shows like *Broad City* and *Fleabag* and performers like Lady Gaga and Rhianna who have paved the way for those of us who work in horror and science fiction to write about the female body not as an accident of nature or outside the Aristotelian norm but to claim an equal space in terms of how our body betrays us or gratifies us or horrifies or amuses us, and have it finally be literature, rather than ghettoized as erotica (for those who don't identify as erotic writers), or putting ourselves in the way of unwanted attention.

And I should say that it's not just women on the stage who have helped pull down the barriers to gender, but women in our own field like **Kathe Khoja** and Livia Lewellyn, and men too. Stephen King with *Carrie* and David Cronenberg with everything, but maybe especially with *The Brood*. I think it's important for those of us pushing these boundaries today to have that sense of the legacy we carry in order for us to pass it onto future generations.

There is today an ongoing debate around the word "genre" in the science fiction/horror milieu. Some agree with Ursula K. Le Guin that it is socially prejudiced; others claim that it is an essential and necessary literary "identity." What is your position on the subject? What determines your choice for these genres?
I don't think it doesn't exist. I also think that it is entirely nonessential, except of course when it works to my advantage! I love calling my work horror when it gets included in Year's Best or anthologies. I am proud of being seen as a horror writer when that occurs, but it doesn't always and more than once I've been told that a story I am putting forward into that category "isn't really horror." Also, as a writer who consistently smooches horror and science

fiction, and dark fantasy against noir and so on, I'm not sure it's essential at all. I know that some of my readers are left wanting if they expected a stronger science fiction theme or a stronger horror theme in a story or novel that begins a certain way, but others are carried along by the character who has no idea she's in a horror novel, or a novel at all, or that there is going to be a science fiction twist at the halfway mark, and what's more she couldn't give a good goddam. Like the rest of us she's just trying to survive past the last page, so my aim is to engage my readers at the level of stakes rather than genre.

I do see the essential library category argument, and I dig seeing the horror and science fiction shelves mobbed by hungry readers, and in the end, I trust them to know what they want. And if we need genre to help that process, I'm fine with that. But I also kind of miss a time, before the evil demon of market categories ruled the world, when Mary Shelley and Coleridge could be on the same table of contents.

Did you choose the genres of horror and science fiction, or did they choose you?
As I indicated above, a bit of both. I was a book nerd back in my woodsy loner days and I read anything and everything, gradually gravitating more and more to Poe and Bradbury, to Shirley Jackson and Angela Carter, King and William Gibson and Shelley and the Brontës, rather than, say, Jane Austen or Zadie Smith or Ian McEwan. Not that I still don't read widely—I think you have to, and I love to—but, as both a reader and a writer, I find refuge in fiction at the far reaches of reality.

The 1960s and 70s are perhaps the most influential decades in the study of gender in speculative fiction. Not only was there an influx of female speculative fiction writers, but also many of these writers applied feminist theory to speculative fiction (Ursula K. Le Guin, Angela Carter, etc.). At the same time, the emergence of African-American female voices brought to light the intersectionality between gender and race. It is as if speculative fiction genres offered better than others the opportunity to challenge social conventions and especially gender and to explore alternative sexualities and alliances. Is it the case in your work? Have you been influenced by specific writers of this generation? What renders speculative fiction

genres apt to engage in sexual politics? How are these genres modified in order to accommodate contemporary post-identitarian claims?

I agree that there has never been a better time than now to inhabit the intersections between gender, race, class, and the fantastic in fiction. The best speculative fiction is in the hands of a wide spectrum of writers whose interests and influences are as diverse as they are. I'm not sure if speculative fiction offers better opportunities to challenge social conventions. I think it really depends on the author. Whatever subversive opportunities exist in speculative fiction, I think they lie in its long history of destabilizing the oppositions upon which consensual reality is constructed. But again, it depends on the author, and as you say, the context that allows a literature of cognitive dissonance, whether in terms of gender, culture, or class, to flourish, and sometimes most resonantly and dangerously—as we are seeing now in the US—against the grain.

Angela Carter and Le Guin are two influences on my work, as is Joanna Russ, and Shirley Jackson, but in part, my writing draws from more recent influences like Kathy Acker, Toni Morrison, Sandra Cisneros, Linda Hogan, Kelly Link, Karen J. Fowler, Kate Bernheimer, Mary Gaitskill, Joyce Carol Oates, Dorothy Allison, Caitlin R. Kiernan, and **Kathe Koja** among others, as well as my own experience and history. I don't know how the genres have been modified to accommodate post-identitarian claims, because my reading of even the most radical and subversive fiction, from Carter to Gaitskill to Kiernan, was never in terms of identity politics but in terms of a general skepticism toward labels of any kind. The politics of difference, the aesthetics of defamiliarization, the poetics of identification can still be in play without labels, and part of the dynamics of resistance in speculative fiction rests on its resistance to identitarian terms. The power of much of today's speculative fiction, although certainly not all, is to embrace, trickster style, undecidability rather than trying to reduce it. Othering, in the fiction I admire and try to write, begins at home, with the self.

In horror fiction, transgressive sexualities are meant to tame the uncanniness, to exorcize sexuality's threat to the self by weaving it into the trauma of horror. Did the enhancement of social acceptability recalibrate what startles, horrifies, or repulses either readers or characters? Did it address the need of structurally modifying the invention of alternative worlds?

I never thought about that—the function of body and sexuality to weave threat into the trauma of horror—I guess that there is an element of that in some horror fiction, to make the threat of the deviant body or desires, say, a part of the horror, but I guess my approach is to see it as a way out of the horror, if anything. I like to think that desensitizing readers to diversity is part of our project in order to wake them up to truly horrifying and repulsive realities.

But sure, social acceptability has given publishers and editors more confidence in taking on diverse voices, because there is a renewed interest in hearing, in reading what these voices have been yelling, singing, growling, howling the whole time. I just write the truth as I approach it, warily, lustfully, traumatically. Shock and revulsion in my work is less a function of body or desire, than the function of language, or of narrative—the power of Shirley Jackson's excessively conforming characters to shock is testament to the danger of fetishizing nonconformity for shock value. The danger of marking deviance is that everything else remains unmarked, normalized, the standard by which monstrosity is measured, and that scares me. My physically or sexually transgressive characters are all me. In my fiction, I've had a transsexual alien obsessed with cock, a ghost who fucks anything that moves, runaway survival sex, a bromance between a Rhodesian Ridgeback called Clint Eastwood and a scungy pierced loner—none are as repulsive or horrifying as the powers vested in shutting down the transformative potential of art.

The wonderful thing about alternative worlds as you say is their adaptability to social change—the worlds invented by Le Guin resonate differently than the worlds of Heinlein. The worlds of Victor LaValle speak a truth that leaves Lovecraft behind. Atwood recalibrates Orwell; Stephen Graham Jones reconfigures *The Howling*—**Angela Slatter** lovingly breathes new life into Angela Carter, and so on. It's the nature of the beast, I guess.

There has been a revival of speculative fiction genres in 2010s and especially with the 2016 electoral victory of Donald Trump. The immediate success of the tv series *Handmaid's Tale*, based on Margaret Atwood's dystopian novel, is indicative. What is the function of speculative fiction literature under the Trump

administration, given that it destabilizes the settled and normative meanings of sex, gender, power, race, etc.? Has this influenced your own writing and in what ways?

I agree that the function of anti-realist literature under Trump is to shine a light on the destructive fictions that got him elected in the first place. But speculative fiction can work to shore up as well as tear down norms, as we know. What I'm interested in is the use of propaganda as a memory wipe, conspiracy theories as bread and circuses to keep folks busy while the structures of power pick their pockets and their souls—I guess that's what's interesting to me. My new novel, *The Bridge*, deals with the harnessing of ideology as a feint. It revolves around a patriarchal Paradise cult that is mainly smoke and mirrors while the slumbering will to power regroups in order to take on a life of its own, the monster of indifference created because it could be.

The several subcategories that emerged with regard to speculative fiction (gay, lesbian, transgender, feminist, black, Philippine), enhanced by the different anthologies that we can find in the market, not only signify the portrayal of specific identities or communities, but also they seem to address every time a specific audience. Do you write/edit/publish with a gendered audience in mind? Do you think that speculative fiction works are differently structured when addressed to traditionally under-portrayed individuals or communities? Is the portrayal of a minority specifically addressed to those that feel portrayed in these works?

I don't write with a gendered audience in mind, or a specific audience, and I'm wondering if the dual purpose of the anthologies you mention is to include both the under-represented readers unable up until now to find themselves in speculative fiction, as well as more mainstream readers in the urgent hope of changing minds and hearts. At their best these anthologies include all readers, to show us a new place, a portal into difference, where we can all go on together. I don't know where, but that's part of the fun, part of the danger and the hope. I do think that there are ways to structure works that address certain communities in certain stories such as some by Silvia Morena-Garcia, Ken Liu, the late Toni Morrison, Laura Mauro, Stephen Graham Jones, Gabino Iglesias, and so many authors who harness the particular in collision with the general— whose writing can be coded (structurally, linguistically, figuratively) to resonate in different ways depending on the reader. Fiction, like desire, wants what it wants. I think that many speculative fiction writers trust in the humanity of their readers to find a piece of themselves, for better or for worse in all of the characters—to other themselves, and defamiliarize the everyday. As speculative fiction writers, we have our specific tools of the trade, but in the end, we're chaotically bound by the transformative potential of worlds and words.

Do you see genre as a symbolic prison or as a space of freedom?
When I think about it, which is rare, I see it as a space of freedom. Any constraints are a red flag to me and I run at them with everything I've got. Plus, I think that there are some so-called conventions of genre that simply make us better writers. Like not showing the monster, the threat, all at once. That forces a novice writer, as we've all been, to write better. The convention of introducing the element of wonder in science fiction—no matter how dystopic—forces our imagination to work so hard it hurts, and anything that hurts in writing has got to be good.

You have chosen to settle down in Australia. Can you feel a difference in your position as a female writer here compared to the United States?
Not really. Australia is a small country and there is an impression at conferences and so on, of a lot of women in genre writing, from authors to publishers and editors, but that could just be an impression. There are of course giants here in speculative fiction writing like Terry Dowling and Garth Nix, but overall, the impression I have in Australia is of a network of very supportive, collegial, talented women with international networks that they are more than willing to share. This exists in the US of course, and you only have to mention the name **Ellen Datlow**, the most influential figure in horror and speculative fiction in the US today, whose generosity and contribution to the culture of speculative fiction, both in terms of its gender politics and its dissemination, cannot be overestimated. As I said earlier, maybe it's a good time to be a female writer right now, and for that I gratefully acknowledge the hard-working pioneers who courageously and sometimes thanklessly carved out this space for us. Knowing this enables me never to glibly see myself as "just" a writer, either here or in the US. The

limitations of gender, class, color, sexual identity, geographical displacement, trauma, religion and so on are real, all the more terrifying so for being the perception of some and not others. Radical possibilities exist in acknowledging a world of limitations and integrating them into better, more truthful fictions.

Have some women authors especially influenced you? Would you "genderize" your influences or consider them as a unisex whole?
More women have influenced me than I can say. Everyone from Shelley to Angela Carter to **Angela Slatter** to Emily Dickinson to Patty Smith to Lady Gaga and Solange and the talented women writing horror today. As I've written about elsewhere, the pioneering women in what was seen as a revisioning of "weird" around 2010–12: Kelly Link, Karen Joy Fowler, Karen Russell and others were a direct influence on my writing not so much in terms of style but in terms of vision. I saw the world as they saw it, and reading their fiction gave me the courage to believe my own eyes. Others inspire me—Amelia Gray, **Gemma Files**, Sarah Langan are a revelation. **Kathe Koja**—the list goes on. Nadia Bulkin, Marina Enriquez. Although not direct influences, the rigor, guts, and beauty of their prose inspires and terrifies me. Shirley Jackson's influence has been monumental but mostly in terms of the perfection of her writing and the control of her rage. And not of course not just women writing in horror or speculative fiction, but women in literature generally. Joyce Carol Oates, Elisabeth Bishop, A. M. Holmes. And in music . . . Joan Jett!

But no, in a word. I would never genderize my influences or my inspirations. When it comes to my literary crushes, I'm an equal opportunity heart emoji.

You have written two novels, *American Monster* and *Aletheia*, in which the main characters are "altered" women. In *American Monster*, Norma is a demon-cyborg, and in *Aletheia*, Thettie becomes a monstrous ghost. Was this a conscious choice, with an intended symbolic charge?
Yes, of course. Thettie and Norma were characters before I wrote about them, so I had very little to do with making them into what they already were—I know that sounds coy, but characters tend to know who they are before you do, although sometimes the relationship is a painful, treacherous process, fraught with betrayal

and misunderstanding. Once we came to some kind of trust, both Norma and Thettie allowed me to layer or encrypt other symbolic coding onto their actions and trajectories, but the charge is not always as intentional as I would like to claim credit for. I did not know that Norma would fall in love with Gene, although I knew that Raye would get under her skin. I didn't exactly know how Thettie came to be a ghost, but when it happened, after I got over the trauma, it seemed obvious. And so whatever symbolic arrows that unleashed, and however they hit their mark or didn't, I really have process, more than intent, to thank for it.

In *Collision*, your latest collection, all stories belong to a different genre, from urban horror to gothic and science fiction. Is this a deliberate choice or is it the way you see yourself as a writer, free from categories?
The latter, very much so, although I definitely love a challenge. So, for instance, if I'm called upon to write a story for a themed anthology, I love trying to keep within those constraints, while coming up with something surprising and new. But generally, if, as an artist, you can't see yourself as free to populate all possible worlds with your imaginings, knowing of course that you'll leave a little bit of yourself behind, then what's the point? I think writing changes us, if we go where our characters go, and carves little pieces off our egos, a process that cuts dangerously close to our hearts— when it comes to genre, my preference is to live dangerously.

CHAPTER FOUR

V. Castro

V. Castro (born in 1979) is a Mexican-American horror writer living in the UK. Notable works: *Goddess of Filth* (novel, 2020), *Mestiza Blood* (novella, 2022).

Dear V. Castro, thank you very much for accepting to be part of this volume, which will focus specifically on the notions of "gender" and "genre." In this light, can you tell us about your background and how this, in your eyes, influenced the person and the writer you are today?

Thank you so much for the opportunity. I am a Mexican-American woman born and raised in Texas. In my late twenties I relocated to the UK.

Both these things have influenced me, because I have seen the lives of generations of women in my family including my great grandmother who was a migrant field worker. My mother was a domestic worker then went to law school in her forties.

Europe and travel have expanded my worldview.

I know what it is like to be a woman of color trying to make it in an industry that has been dominated by cis white males. Even now the scales are not balanced.

Every experience, great and small, challenges me and inspires me. Yes, at times it has been difficult to persevere, but I do so because I want my own daughter to know different.

Do you or did you ever feel any gendered resistance in the milieu or in the reviews?
I don't read reviews unless I am tagged. It doesn't just belong to me, and I don't care what people think. I can't. If it's out there, it's public domain.

Did you encounter any discrimination specifically related to your gender in your writing career?
Probably, but in publishing a lot of that happens behind the scenes and you don't know for certain. However, the historical lack of representation points to yes, it's even worse if you are a woman of color.

Do you feel that "genre" literature, and especially horror, is looked down upon by the establishment?
Absolutely, even though people love thrillers, there is a lot of real horror in those books. Most people think horror has to only be about monsters or the man hiding with a knife. What is good about horror now is that we are including more voices to expand the definition and this includes more women.

What writers have you been influenced by? Was their gender important to you?
Growing up there were pretty much no Latinx horror writers and very few women I knew of. So, I was influenced by Alvin Schwartz and later Stephen King. There was Shirley Jackson and Mary Shelley, but that was it. Gender wasn't important until I realized how unrepresented we were. As a kid those things don't register.

The Latinx writers were writing in the literary field (Anya and Allende). That is why I work so hard in what I do. I love it but I hope it changes the landscape for the better.

You write horror and a mix of horror and erotica. What is determinant in your choice of these genres?
It all depends on the story I envision telling. If the story progresses to include sex, then I absolutely will. I am very much a go-with-the-flow storyteller. Usually, I write from a very organic state.

What do you think renders horror genres apt to engage in sexual politics?
Because typically women have been targets of the most brutal aspects of horror. Many women are reclaiming this space and changing the narratives.

You are of "Chicano" background and clearly define your identity on the cover and themes of all your books. How do you feel about the general atmosphere of polarization about "race" and "culture" going on at the moment? Do you feel that your writing and your identity as a woman can have an impact on these topics?
There is only polarization because we are finally demanding what we deserve instead of accepting the situation. We have been ignored and whitewashed for years, and now is the time for us to be bold. It is important we demand our place because no one will give it to us.

The several subcategories that emerged with regard to horror (gay, lesbian, transgender, feminist, black, Latinx, etc.), enhanced by the different anthologies that we can find in the market, not only signify the portrayal of specific identities or communities, but also each of them seems to address a specific audience. Do you write/edit/ publish with a gendered audience in mind?
I edited a book entitled *Latinx Screams* a few years ago because for a very long time anthologies were *only* of cis white men. That was it. And things slowly changed; however, Latinx writers were still very much overlooked. I wanted an outlet for our voices, hence the title. Yes, I write with women of color in mind because we are still very behind when it comes to horror.

Do you think that horror works are differently structured when addressed to traditionally under-portrayed individuals or communities? And, is the portrayal of a minority specifically addressed to those that feel portrayed in these works?
Horror and literature are different in general because the story might not be reliant on stereotypes or harmful tropes. When I write I am addressing everyone through my own lens, but I happen to be a Latina with a certain set of experiences. It is up to the reader to relate to it or not. Another Latina may read it and feel it doesn't address them. Everyone digests a story differently.

In your novels, *Goddess of Filth* and *Queen of the Cicadas,* as well as in many stories from your collection *Mestiza Blood,* your main characters are all women that reconnect with a mythical supernatural figure from their cultural past. Do you consider this as a political and feminist message for all women, or do you aim particularly at empowering women with a Latinx background?

I want my work to be for everyone; however, I especially want to be a storyteller who speaks to women of color because we have been ignored for so long. Representation and inclusion are not just about having a diverse cast of characters in a story, it's about someone who has lived that life, that identity, and was given the space to talk about it. My hope is that other people will be inspired to tell their own stories in their true authentic voice.

The Aztec goddess present in your books and stories, Mictēcacihuātl, is the goddess of death. You have therefore chosen a direct opposite of the traditional symbolic attributes of womanhood, which are, in our Western culture, birth and life. Yet, she is not "evil," as a white writer could have portrayed her, but, on the contrary, attached to justice and benevolent to those who worship her. Have you consciously used her terrifying figure to attack colonial prejudices about first-nation cultures?

Yes, absolutely. It's a disgusting fact my ancestors were called savages when the colonizers had their own version of brutality. There are entire tribes of human beings who no longer exist because of colonialism.

And many people do not know about the older deities. That is a shame.

Sexuality is very central in all of your books and stories and you even have a vampire series that is explicitly erotic. After the #metoo wave, do you feel that genre literature can push forward a more balanced, albeit provocative, depiction of female sexuality? Do you feel that your books offer a possibility of sexual liberation for your readers?

It's about time women and everyone have an opportunity to speak about their sexuality. Genre fiction has always carried certain stereotypes and tropes that have been harmful to women and other marginalized groups. Now that can change. It is changing.

I often have women thanking me for my honest description of sex and also being sex-work-, body-, and sex-positive.

CHAPTER FIVE

Ellen Datlow

Ellen Datlow (born in 1949) is an award-winning American horror, science fiction, and fantasy editor. Notable publications: *Screams in the Dark* (anthology, 2022), *Best Horror of the Year* (anthology, 2021).

Thank you very much for accepting to answer these few questions. This book is going to focus specifically on the notions of "gender" and "genre" as we believe that they are closely related, by their question of definition and identities. Before we dig deeper on these topics, can you tell us about your background and how this, in your eyes, influenced the person and editor you are today?
I've read science fiction, fantasy, and horror since I was a child. My parents encouraged me to read. We always had books around the apartments we lived in, and my mother took me to the library on a regular basis, allowing me to read anything I chose to.

I went to SUNY at Albany and majored in English Literature, mostly because of my love of reading. My options once I graduated were to teach, work in a library (which I did while at university), work in a bookstore, or go into publishing. I knew nothing about the latter until I actually got my first publishing job around 1973 at Little, Brown & Company in New York.

I worked in mainstream/trade book publishing for about five years and for several different publishing houses. Working in book publishing, I learned a lot about publishing in general, even though I wasn't then working in genre. One reason was that I still wanted to keep my options open and was afraid that if I worked for a science fiction/fantasy book publisher, I'd be pigeon-holed forever. The other was that my perception was that most science fiction novels were originally published in the science fiction/fantasy magazines and so were not commissioned or acquired or edited by book editors. That might have been a misconception; I'm honestly not sure.

But even then, while working in mainstream publishing, I did some freelance reading for the SF Book Club, Dell Publishing, and Ace, in addition to reading for Book of the Month Club and Twentieth Century Fox.

Do you feel there is still a gender-oriented differentiation among genres, both in the writers' represented gender and in the choice of the genre?

Overall, my perception is that fewer men *or* women are writing science fiction. Fantasy and what might be termed "speculative fiction" is more prevalent these days. But from what I can tell, my answer to your question is no.

In the horror field, there are definitely more women writing horror than ever before—and both the output and acclaim for their work has been expanding exponentially annually.

Do you think women in horror and science fiction are in a better position today than when you began to work in publishing, in the early 1980s? Do you feel any gendered resistance in the milieu or in the reviews?

Oh yes. Certainly, in horror, something with which I'm more familiar. The way I judge this is by what I select for my annual *Best Horror of the Year*. Initially, when I started co-editing a best of the year in 1987, with the other editor covering fantasy, there was a preponderance of men in my Table of Content. Over the past thirty years, this has changed—the ratio of male to female becoming almost equal. In 2008, there were four women in the Table of Content and seventeen men. In 2019, there were nine stories by women, twelve by men, and one by a nonbinary contributor. In 2020, there are nine stories by women, fifteen stories and a poem by men.

In the early 1980s and 90s, several women came to prominence in science fiction/fantasy publishing books and magazines: Beth Meacham, Susan Allison, Betsy Wollheim, Judy Lynn Del Rey, Betsy

Mitchell, me, Shawna McCarthy, and others. This was after the 1940s through 60s when mostly men ran the genre lines in publishing.

This is not to say that there weren't still plenty of male editors.

There was initially some pushback, indicated by smarmy remarks by a few male writers. And the occasional misogynist has always existed, railing against women "invading" their field.

I experienced a few isolated incidents during my career in short fiction editing. But these incidents were merely drunken petulance for the most part. It was not discrimination because the crucial thing is: We had the power, we held the purse strings so of course those few, whiny male writers had to come around or they wouldn't be selling to us.

Once I started working at *OMNI* (my first magazine job) and became fiction editor (after being associate fiction editor for a year and a half), there was an annoying incident less related to my gender than to the fact that I didn't come up from genre publishing, and the male in question was resentful that he was not chosen to be fiction editor (which is laughable, because the publisher had no idea who he was). But again, I was in a unique position in that *OMNI* was the highest-paying genre fiction market, which means I had power, so that everyone wanted to sell stories to me.

Did you encounter any discrimination specifically related to your gender in your editing career?
I didn't feel that, no. In book publishing it was "class" discrimination. If you didn't have an Ivy League education, you were not given the same opportunities and were often passed over and/or not taken seriously.

This question will be more apt when asked of writers *because* editors are in a position of power.

There is today an ongoing debate around the word "genre" in the speculative fiction/horror milieu. Some agree with Ursula K. Le Guin that it is socially prejudiced; others claim that it is an essential and necessary literary "identity."

What is your position on the subject?
I have no interest in such a debate. As far as I'm concerned, genre is merely a marketing tool, no more no less.

This "debate" has been ongoing for decades. There are those who would ghettoize anything not considered "mainstream," although mainstream is as much a genre as mystery, science fiction, fantasy, and horror. What I've always found fascinating is how eager some people working and reading in the fields of science fiction/fantasy/horror are so quick to dismiss work that is published as mainstream, but which is actually science fiction/fantasy/horror. The prejudice goes both ways.

The 1960s and 70s are perhaps the most influential decades in the study of gender in speculative fiction and horror. Not only was there an influx of female writers, but also many of these writers applied feminist theory to speculative fiction (Ursula K. Le Guin, Angela Carter, Shirley Jackson, etc.). At the same time, the emergence of African-American female voices brought to light the intersectionality between gender and race. It is as if speculative fiction and horror genres offered better than others the opportunity to challenge social conventions, especially gender, and to explore alternative sexualities and alliances.

I was not working in the science fiction or horror fields until the early 1980s so anything I say on the subject is speculation and my backward-looking perception of the period. I am not an academic, I can only use my reading experience during that period of time.

I don't know what you mean by "applied feminist theory"—if you mean that much of their fiction presented a feminist point of view or were written from a female perspective then yes, certainly some of the former and most of the latter, although not always.

As for African-American female voices emerging during that period, the only two I'm aware of were Octavia E. Butler in science fiction and Jewell Gomez in horror. If there were others, I'm afraid I was and am still unaware of them.

Science fiction has always been the perfect genre for speculation—that's the point of it: envisioning other worlds, other ways of life—so for me it's disappointing that more male writers in the past didn't use the opportunity to speculate more about gender.

There has been relatively little actual exploration of gender in science fiction. John Varley did some excellent work regarding gender in some of his stories (e.g., "Options"), and of course Joanna

Russ, Ursula Le Guin, and James Tiptree, Jr., were major voices dealing with gender. But aside from them, I'm not aware of others. There had been a couple of early "erotic science fiction" anthologies but they were not actually about gender relations. It wasn't until my 1990 anthology *Alien Sex*, which despite the title is about male-female-other gender relations that there seems to have been much focus on the subject. Half the stories were reprints and included provocative fiction about gender by James Tiptree, Jr., Connie Willis, Leigh Kennedy, among others.

What, in your eyes, renders speculative fiction and horror genres apt to engage in sexual politics?
i already answered about speculative fiction above.

There is so much real-life horror perpetrated against women that it's natural for women writers to push back against those tropes of the helpless, victimized female.

The several subcategories that emerged with regard to speculative fiction and horror (gay, lesbian, transgender, feminist, black, etc.), enhanced by the different anthologies that we can find in the market, not only signify the portrayal of specific identities or communities, but also each of them seems to address a specific audience. Do you edit and publish with a gendered audience in mind?
No, I do not.

Do you think that speculative fiction and horror stories are differently structured when addressed to traditionally under-portrayed individuals or communities?
Structured differently? No.

When working on anthology, do you seek a balance between genders in the authors you are presenting?
Initially, I attempt to achieve a balance by who I solicit for stories. But writers don't always come through with stories. Life gets in the way, they don't have an idea they like for a theme anthology, or I don't like the submission enough to accept it. So as submissions come in, I'm always aware if one of my anthologies starts becoming heavily weighted toward one gender over another. At a certain point, I might solicit a few more stories from writers of the other gender.

You have also published a number of theme-centered anthologies, but none, it seems, centered on women authors only. Is that a voluntary choice?
Absolutely, yes.

Do you feel that "genre" matters today? What would be its strengths and challenges compared to "high-brow" literature?
The genres of science fiction/fantasy/horror matter as much as they ever did. Its strength is that these genres take more chances in every way than most so-called "literature." They take imaginative leaps and/or delve into the dark of human existence. The only challenge is to remain fresh, to encourage new voices with different experiences. No different than "high-brow" literature.

CHAPTER SIX

Gemma Files

Gemma Files (born in 1968) is an award-winning Canadian horror writer. She is also a film critic and a journalist. Notable works: *Experimental Film* (novel, 2015), *In That Endlessness, Our End* (collection, 2021).

Dear Gemma Files, thank you very much for accepting to be part of this volume, which will focus specifically on the notions of "gender" and "genre". In this light, can you tell us about your background and how this, in your eyes, influenced the person and the writer you are today? Do you feel any gendered resistance in the milieu or in the reviews?
When I first began placing my writing, which was ... in the mid-1990s, I think ... there were far fewer women writing horror in general; it was definitely the exception rather than the rule, or at least looked on as such. Add to that the fact that my early stuff was very heavily influenced by people like Clive Barker, **Kathe Koja**, Skipp and Spector, Billy Martin (then Poppy Z. Brite), etc., and there was a certain amount of kickback which I wouldn't necessarily have identified as being due to my gender, except for the fact that it often seemed couched in a sort of surprise or revulsion that, as a woman, I chose to write this sort of stuff. I wrote for myself, the way I still do, and back then I was far angrier and hornier than I am today, with my rage fueling my sexual expression and vice versa. Not everybody was going to like the stories I told, so I wasn't too surprised whenever that happened.

For example: I remember at least one review of the story "Kiss of Fire" (later republished in *Kissing Carrion*), which struck me as almost obsessive in its pearl-clutching over the fact that it contained a male-on-male rape Then, "I wasn't trying to apologize about it, but I had described it in detail and in a way . . . horrified by his own behavior while he enjoyed a lot, in a purely physical way, committing said crime." I was a bit taken aback by this, since in my brain, I'd simply labeled "Kiss of Fire" as an experiment in James Ellroy pastiche; seen from *that* angle, I felt its content was about the same as I'd found thus far in any given Ellroy book. But then I decided "screw it," and stuck that particular review in a collection of negative criticism of my work that I used to make myself laugh and feel better about myself, I'd modeled it after the hilarious "bad reviews only" quotes on the back of a British copy of J. G. Ballard's *Crash* I picked up right after I graduated from university.

One thing I know about myself, probably because I'm neuroatypical, is that if I don't watch out, I tend to easily obsess over the idea that I'm not good enough/not doing things the way I "should," etc. So, I had to train myself to respond to negative reviews with a hearty "Agree to disagree, I guess"; I note that stuff, and then move on. Though I will say that my favorite recent bad reviews definitely do still seem a bit gendered, when I think about them—from the dudes on Reddit who think my stuff is too flowery (i.e., female) to the women who think I'm a bad mother because of things I have my main character in *Experimental Film* say about her son. Oh, or the guy who said of my latest collection: "Some of these stories I liked and other ones were 'meh,' but ALL of them were better than *Experimental Film*." What I've found is that since the majority of genre readers often tend to assume the default setting unless told otherwise (i.e., that all stories are told from a white, cis, straight, male, American perspective. Whenever you drop in information that tells them they're wrong, at least *some* of them will respond as if you just pulled some sort of nasty trick on them: *Why's this gotta be so gay, man? Why you gotta rub my face in stuff I didn't sign up for? Ew, lady parts!* Or, whatever.

So, was I sometimes treated weirdly because I was a woman writing the stuff I write/have written? Have I felt crowded out or talked over, ignored? Did I suffer professionally? Yes, I think so. I think I might have not connected with some editors and publishers because of gender issues; I think I might have been misconstrued because (in part) of gender issues, allied with the fact that I sometimes overshare and hyperfixate on things in ways even other nerds find off-putting. But then again, I think I might not have noticed that as much as some other people, because of all the other things I had going on—the fact that I thought of myself as a brain on top of a spine for a long time, the fact that (even now) I don't read social cues the way neurotypical people do, the fact that I used to get blackout drunk in public to get over my social anxiety. There are as many women as men I haven't connected with, from that angle. Not to mention how I've let people get away with quite amazing things in retrospect, both socially and professionally, because I thought of them as friends, and that friendship meant more to me than allowing myself to feel insulted or minimized by their statements or behavior. Because, on some level, I have a tape in the back of my head which tells me I'm so dislikable and hard to handle that I should feel lucky to have any friends at all, even when those friends don't treat me as well as I'd like to be treated.

What I'm saying, I suppose, is that when I was younger, this sort of stuff mainly bounced off me, much like any idea that the creepy dude who sought me out at a con once because I'd written a story about autoerotic asphyxiation just so that he could breathlessly recommend *The General's Daughter* to me might be a threat, rather than an annoyance. And now that I'm older, I just don't care; I'm going to keep on doing what I'm doing, no matter who doesn't like it, no matter for what reason. This is where being Aspergian comes in handy, I suppose.

There is today an ongoing debate around the word "genre" in the science fiction/horror milieu. Some agree with Ursula K. Le Guin that it is socially prejudiced; others claim that it is an essential and necessary literary "identity." What is your position on the subject?
I mean . . . genre is essentially a category, but having categories is useful, especially when you're looking for more of something you respond to. You can't leave it all to algorithms. I do think it registers on a cultural level as being "less than," when compared to (say) Literature with a big L, but what else are you going to call it? *Everything* outside the nonfiction section is fiction. I've defined myself as a horror writer for so long that I almost don't know what else I would call myself, if someone told me that this option had

been taken off the table; something with "dark" in it, I guess, as a descriptor. Just so nobody gets misled.

You write horror. What is determinant in your choice of this genre? How do you think it allowed you more freedom to express yourself than traditional literature?
Because horror is a ghetto inside a ghetto inside a ghetto, a place where nobody ends up unless they really want to be there, it sort of means that you don't have to warn people they might see something that will shock them. Simply knowing you don't have to worry about making your perspective characters "likable" can be spectacularly freeing; in the same way, sometimes, I find myself thinking up a particular twist and going: "Oh, that would be *awful*," then laughing to myself. Similarly, while I used to say, "The great thing about horror is that you can kill everybody," these days I'd add the caveat ". . . if you want to." Overall, I feel in my gut that horror suits me best because a) it deals with the full range of universal emotions, from the dreadful to the numinous, and without darkness for contrast and context we wouldn't know what light *was*, and b) because it allows me to describe truly awful things in weirdly beautiful terms, which is my jam.

I also love monsters, because I spent a long time thinking I was one. Many of my stories embrace the idea of "monster pride" . . . the thesis that it's not who/what we are that makes us better or worse, it's the choices we make, the actions we choose to carry out. Horror, to me, is about trying to understand the things society tells us are inexplicable, finding empathy for the things (and people) we're most repulsed by, or want to separate ourselves from completely. In that particular way, I believe it's directly opposed to the comforting idea that there's an "us" versus a "them," that some human beings can either give up their humanity through what they do or be deprived of their humanity by being labeled inhuman. We're all capable of everything; people do, will do exactly what they think they can get away with for as long as they're allowed to; all morality is practical. The only thing we can ever do, as Captain Kirk so beautifully put it, is to say "we're not going to kill . . . *today*!" Then try to keep to that promise, even though we know we might find ourselves in circumstances that make that sadly improbable.

So many of today's problems seem to stem from people being told that thinking about bad things makes them happen, because it means that when those bad things inevitably DO happen anyhow, their whole worldview is completely undermined: *Oh shit, God hates me and it's the End of Times? I guess I can just throw conventional standards of behavior right out the window!* Horror not only taught me what I can survive, but how I'm willing to survive it; it confirmed my belief that being kind in the face of cruelty is the easiest way to give a perverse, passive-aggressive sort of "fuck you" to evil. I think that's useful. No one can persuade me otherwise.

What writers have you been influenced by? Was their gender important to you?
All writing begins in pastiche, so when I first started writing, it was in complete imitation of the people whose styles I felt most attracted to. Did it matter to me if the writers I was imitating were male or female? Not until after a certain point in my life, I think . . . maybe I started noticing it and responding to it as a plus if a writer was female around the time I turned eighteen, which was also when I started noticing if directors of movies I loved were female—Kathryn Bigelow for *Near Dark*, for example. Tanith Lee taught me that I could write about queer stuff and queer people and also write things that absolutely were fantasy, dark or not; Clive Barker taught me that being poetic, florid, and using words that were not so big or specific were things you could absolutely do while writing horror. Stephen King taught me that I could root my writing in personal experience without feeling like I was tethered to it—like I was writing "a fucking Oprah's Book Club selection," as I snapped at my mom, once. **Koja**, Brite, and Kiernan taught me that there was no such thing as "too far." And, all the people I admire taught me that I could write epic shit about whatever I felt like writing about, because all anybody could do about it was refuse to publish it— they certainly couldn't stop me.

It goes the same way for me writing my share of fan fiction, actually, without which I probably never would have made the leap from writing increasingly lengthy "short" stories to writing genuine chaptered narratives/novels and novellas. And, I suppose that since fan fiction is mainly recognized as an inherently "female" variety of fan-work, then you could say that the gender of the people I learned from in *that* particular area mattered to me. But then again, I'm a slasher from way back, having fantasized about various male characters introduced to me by popular culture getting it on with each other since long before I even knew there was a name for the phenomenon. It's still hilarious to me that my life has gone from having to explain this fetish to people who were *dumbstruck* at the very concept at age eighteen to tripping across the received internet wisdom that "oh yeah, all girls like yaoi" everywhere by the time I was thirty. Still, if I hadn't spent almost a year writing nothing but fanfic about James Mangold's *3:10 to Yuma* to cheer myself up after my son was diagnosed, I wouldn't have written either *A Book of Tongues* or any of the rest of my Hexslinger series. That's not debatable. It was an incredibly important part of my personal development as a writer, and the fact that it seemed like a "safe space" for those who identified as female to be honest about their desires certainly had something to do with it.

As a professional, meanwhile, I'm continuously influenced by the standards set by all sorts of people, both male- and female-identified. The incredible strength of will I see manifested in trans writers who live their lives in the open, out and proud; the ever-spreading spectrum of identification I see in writers that Old Lady Me keeps wanting to call "queer"; the increasing prevalence of writers who are unashamed to write stories filtered through their specific racial and cultural backgrounds ... I'm white-presenting as a sack of sheets, so a lot of what I try to do these days is to sit back, listen, and try not to take up too much space, but I really don't feel diminished in any way by their presence. Them being who they are and owning it is part of what makes me feel free to own my own areas of difference in public.

There are a lot of lesbian, bi, and queer characters in your stories. In your eyes, what makes the horror genre apt to engage in sexual politics?
I'm not sure I'd put it that way. Isn't the fact that people who aren't straight exist inherently political? most of them often exist under political structures which assume they don't (at best) or assume they shouldn't (at worst)? For myself, I know that I made a decision a long time back to shift the default within my own work—not just from mainly straight to mainly gay and bi, as in the Hexslinger tales, but so that it wasn't such "an incredible bag of dicks," as somebody once observed, of *A Book of Tongues*. I mean, westerns—Weird or otherwise—have their patterns, but the last thing I wanted

to do was to create a world, where every woman the reader came across was either a monster, a whore, or both. Not that there's anything wrong with that! And yet . . . there's a whole lot of people out there right now creating very similar worlds, without ever thinking about how they could very easily have done something different.

Yes, horror is to a large extent—by its very nature—about "the Other" . . . the unfamiliar, the unnatural, the different, the Weird. The variant. Yet "monster" derives from "monstrum," a portent of something different. Is *different* always negative? When people say that a protagonist has to be likable, or complain that they can't identify with a character who doesn't share the same characteristics as them, I wonder how they feel so comfortable letting the whole world know that their capacity to care about other people in terrible circumstances goes only so far, no further. How they would ever want to essentially boast about how wizened their own empathy glands must have somehow become, when they can't even suspend their own prejudices for as long as it takes someone to tell them a fucking story.

Or, to put it another way: Horror is where we break the rules, even the rules that tell us who we are, what we do and don't approve of, what people have to be like in order to "deserve" our identification with them. It's where we play out scenarios we'd find extremely threatening in real life, and maybe walk away changed, but only on the inside; that's the *point* of horror. To explore our own darkness, sound it, discover its depths. To figure out what we might be capable of, long before life forces us to confirm those parameters under genuine, nonfictional pressure.

My decision to shift the default goalposts, meanwhile, has allowed me to approach stories from what I find considerably more interesting perspectives. Because I don't necessarily have to worry about the usual patterns of male/female interactions, I'm free not just to write about homosocial relationships but also to criticize them—as in "Grave Goods," for example, which spins off of an older, second-wave feminist archaeology professor's decision to assemble an all-female dig team, on the assumption that they'd "naturally" work better together. Instead, she's confronted, first, by friction between the Indigenous tribal liaison overseeing the dig and the biologist assessing the strange bones they dig up, who happens to be black-presenting, then by her own prejudices when she realizes that our main POV (point of view) character is trans and didn't feel she had to tell anybody that fact before signing up. I guess I could have done some of that with a less vag-heavy cast, but I didn't want to, and I'm proud of the result.

Horror is an historically sex-charged genre, not only through eroticism, but also by presenting queer characters or morally "offensive" situations. Do you think the horror genre today has been modified in order to accommodate contemporary post-identitarian claims, or that it is a natural process which was linked with its nature from the start?
Again, horror is about the Other—our repulsion with it, but also our attraction toward it, an attraction which can easily turn into identification with said Other. Almost all body horror involves the idea of changing until you no longer recognize yourself, which can be either destroying or freeing (or both). The only thing that seems to be changing is that *everyone* now feels free to put themselves in the protagonist's position, no matter how they identify. And you know what? That's cool as hell.

In horror fiction, transgressive sexualities are meant to tame the uncanniness, to exorcize sexuality's threat to the self by weaving it into the trauma of horror. Did the enhancement of social acceptability recalibrate what startles, horrifies, or repulses either readers or characters?
To begin with, that's a fascinating thesis, though I'm not sure I would have ever completely agreed with it. Uncanniness comes from a variety of sources; I'm thinking here about Derek Marlowe's *Nightshade* (1975), in which the main narrator is fairly obviously a deeply closeted homosexual of the oldest possible school—he spends a lot of the book freaking out between the lines over the sexual urges his wife exhibits, straight or otherwise (not to mention toward a *black guy* who *practices voudoun*, ew ew ewwww), because he needs her to remain a pure, childlike creature with whom he can have a completely sexless beard marriage so that he won't be tempted to act on his own "destructive" impulses. The threat here comes from the way he clings desperately to a system of "normality" that brands his own true self and abnormal, totally internalized homophobia. Would this work as well, if the character was straight, under similar circumstances?

These days, there are a lot more overtly queer writers writing overtly queer main characters who've grown up under very different circumstances from those the people of my generation grew up with, yet face similar challenges that can contribute to the horror of their situation(s). They don't have to worry as much about AIDS, but staying closeted is still a deal; they can get married legally, but not everywhere, and hate crimes are very much still happening. Instead of worrying so much about how they perceive themselves and how the world perceives them, these younger writers tend to worry more about consent and communication, about abuse and manipulation, about rape—and when I say that, I'm actually talking about *all* of them. A straight(ish) male writer friend of mine recently told me about how an old girlfriend forced him to have sex with her and he only recently realized that it was rape, and I could sympathize, because I've been date-raped myself. His courage in talking about his traumas gives me courage to talk about mine, and hopefully vice versa.

It can be horrible for a straight woman to feel she "has" to have sex with a straight man just because they're both straight and it's "normal," just like it can be horrible for a queer person of either sex to feel they "have" to have sex with a queer person of either sex just because they're both queer. And because all of us only have so many words to work with when it comes to love and sex anyways, we can all hurt each other a million different ways without even wanting to, disappoint each other, puncture each other's worldviews, destroy each other's hopes and dreams. That's part of horror, too, or should be.

In "genre fiction" such as horror, fantasy, speculative fiction, and other relatively formulaic genres, there seems to be a tension in character identity as well as plot structure and situations between recognizable stereotypes that characterize a genre and facilitate reading, and, on the other hand, the malleability of the imaginary allowed by the construction of alternative universes. How do you manage to negotiate this tension with respect to gender images?

One of the things I've always tried to do is to inhabit characters without judging them, or while only judging them so far as I believe they're able or likely to judge themselves, so that's what I try to do here, no matter the sort of story those characters find themselves inside.

The several subcategories that emerged with regard to horror (gay, lesbian, transgender, feminist, black, etc.), enhanced by the different anthologies that we can find in the market, not only signify the portrayal of specific identities or communities, but also each of them seems to address a specific audience. Do you write with a gendered or sexually-oriented audience in mind?

Not unless I'm asked to. Most of my anthology work these days comes by invitation, and I sort those invitations by my ability to write quickly to the theme. Also, although I've been invited to write for a fair few queer-themed anthologies, I'm essentially functionally straight myself and I don't want to take a slot away from someone who genuinely identifies as such. Similarly, I wouldn't feel as if I could apply to an anthology that was specifically slanted toward giving writers of a particular racial, cultural, or sexual identity a platform unless I was specifically told I could. So, I just write my stuff and if it turns out there are characters who are trans, queer, not white/Christian, whatever in them, then great.

One of the things I've always found interesting about this question of writing characters whose identities don't jibe with your own is that as a cis woman who grew up watching movies and reading books where 90 percent of the characters were usually male, I've never assumed that I should only be prepared to inhabit cis female characters—indeed, at one point, I was told outright that there were "too many" women in my stories and that I should turn some of them into men, if I wanted the stories to be salable (but not gay men, because of many reasons). Similarly, BIPOC writers I know have talked about how they always felt prepared to write white Christian male characters, the same way queer writers talk about how they always felt prepared to write straight characters, or disabled writers felt prepared to write abled characters. The cultural default is simply assumed to be the norm, available to everyone; the rule is the rule, not the exception.

The difference right now is that more and more of us are writing out of our exceptions, because we've realized there's nothing actually wrong with being . . . exceptional, I guess. That, in fact, being exceptional in some way is far more universal than the mainstream makes it look. It doesn't limit your market. It expands it.

Do you think that horror works are differently structured when addressed to traditionally under-portrayed individuals or communities?
For me, the most important thing is to avoid any implication that bad things happen to characters because of their identity rather than because of their choices. It's that simple, and that rule applies both to default and nondefault characters.

Is the portrayal of a minority specifically addressed to those that feel portrayed in these works?
Only so far as I believe that everybody should be able to find themselves in the stories they read. I mean, a queer writer friend of mine recently read my collection *Spectral Evidence*, and was highly ambivalent about the character of Allfair "A-Cat" Chatwin, a pansexual holler witch who shows up in a trio of linked stories ("Crossing the River," "Black Bush," "His Face, All Red"). They noted that A-Cat is both charming and seductive and amoral, not to mention a straight-up magically assisted rapist with an incestuous fixation on her own half-sister. Thankfully, they didn't take it that I was tarring all queer people with the A-Cat brush (#notallhollerwitches), but they were disturbed by her. To me, that's a win; I *mean* A-Cat to be disturbing. She's not a nice lady. Her sexuality doesn't have much to do with that, though, except in that I think most magic-users feel a certain power high that comes with their abilities that makes them frankly not give a fuck what other people think about them. A-Cat certainly uses her sexuality to manipulate the people around her, but she'd do that if she was a) a gay or b) a straight guy. It's just that I've read that story already, a lot.

In many of your short stories, your female protagonists are very often ambivalent, sexually and morally. For instance, you use powerful witches, who are destructive, yet at the same time seem to preserve a sort of "order" through the chaos they provoke. Are these figures archetypes you have voluntarily decided to write about, or are they the result of a less conscious process of creation? In other words, do you use the figure of the witch, queer sexuality included, as a vessel to express your creativity, or has it imposed itself as a subconscious choice?

One of the ways in which witches break the rules—the main reason they're "scary," or have been characterized as such, historically— has always been sexually: They take charge, they have "perverse" sex (which could range from wanting to be on top and/or wanting oral sex to fucking demons and/or stealing men's penises), and they practice birth control. The earliest mention of witches in the Anglo-Saxon legal code comes in reference to "wise women" giving abortions, and the people charged under that law weren't the witches themselves, but those women who patronized them. Often, witches are accused of being not entirely human, so their inherent implied queerness becomes the inherent implied queerness of any other sort of monster, whether or not an individual witch herself is queer. For me, however, it's simply all about freedom—the freedom to do and be whatever, or whoever, you want. It's a very conscious choice.

In your novel *Experimental Film*, you blend the history of cinema with non-Western folklore. The female protagonist finds herself facing a malevolent supernatural being, itself a female, who has been captured on film by a woman occultist. It is very interesting that you mix genre and gender within the notion of "images," blurring all notions at the same time. Would you consider *Experimental Film* as feminist esthetics manifesto?
Sure, maybe. I was definitely interested in the idea of Lois Cairns, Mrs. A. Macalla Whitcomb, and Lady Midday forming a kind of triumvirate, with Lady Midday as the muse who doles out creative inspiration to Mrs. Whitcomb in return for worship, and Mrs. Whitcomb as the muse who leads Lois to Lady Midday, who then tries to set up the same sort of relationship with Lois. Meanwhile, Lois is female because I based her explicitly on myself; Mrs. Whitcomb is female because I was thinking of all the female creators who were present throughout film history but got literally written out of the historical record, which I know a bit about because I taught film history; Lady Midday is female-identified (she's a deity, I'm sure gender works the same way for her) because I've always been fascinated by all the instances of ancient female creator/earth-goddesses supplanted by male sky-gods that recur throughout global mythology. Also, Lois's main conflict in her personal life is about motherhood, so I wanted to pair her up with a mother-goddess of the oldest possible school, utterly utilitarian and ruthless.

But to my mind, it's as much about neurodivergence and internalized ableism as it is about feminism, really—possibly more, since I wrote it during the time when I was really coming to grips with the fact that while my son was diagnosed with autism at three and a half, I've never been diagnosed, even though I display all the basic characteristics of Asperger's Syndrome. This is fairly normal as part of almost any mother's "autism journey," especially since the only explanation for why kids are born neurodivergent that makes sense to me is the genetic one. My son is on the spectrum (medically proven), so it's very likely that I and my husband are both on the spectrum (undiagnosed, but supported by shared symptomatology). You could analyze *Experimental Film* from that angle and come up with just as good a thesis.

Still, I did make decisions which cluster female characters together in a supportive way (Lois as Safie's teacher, Safie as Lois's assistant) as well as an ambivalent way (Lois's mom, who both loves her and undercuts her), and people have pointed out that the character of Wrob Barney being gay as well as antagonistic to Lois's quest through the book might be easily read as homophobic on some level. But then again, I've sometimes gotten props for making Lois's husband Simon supportive of her intellectual drives—another decision I made on a strategic level was that I wasn't interested in having Simon abandon her halfway through, or force her to choose between him, their kid, and her search for Mrs. Whitcomb—and sometimes been criticized for making him a pussy-whipped nonentity. There's a lot going on in that book, and I'm glad.

CHAPTER SEVEN

Elizabeth Hand

Liz Hand (born in 1957) is an American science fiction, horror, and fantasy writer. She is also a reviewer and critic for major American newspapers. Notable works: *Wylding Hall* (novella, 2015), *The Book of Lamps and Banners* (novel, 2020).

Do you think women in horror and fantasy are in a better position today than when you began to write? Do you feel any gendered resistance in the milieu or in the reviews?

I think there are more women writers today, and more opportunities for them to share their work: the Big Five publishers, myriad small presses, digital-only publishers, self-publishing, etc. For the last two years, science fiction, fantasy, and horror awards have been dominated by women writers. A quick glance at a list of science fiction, fantasy, and horror books available for review was split pretty much down the middle, female/male. However, I suspect that male writers still are the majority—I'd love to be wrong about that. I think the fact that we continue to need to ask about gendered resistance speaks to the fact that it exists. I personally haven't felt resistance to my own work, insofar as reviews go, and as a reviewer, I try to cover all kinds of writers, though I am sometimes limited when I'm assigned a book to review. I do try to seek out new writers, especially women, to review.

Did you encounter any discrimination specifically related to your gender in your writing career?

I'm not sure if this qualifies as discrimination, but I began attending conventions in the late 1980s, when I was just starting to publish (my first novel appeared in 1990). For some years, the only panel I would be assigned to at any individual con would be on the topic of feminist science fiction. At some point, a version of "But can women really write science fiction?" might be posed. It reached a point where I would request *not* to be on any panel about women and genre fiction—not because I didn't care about it (obviously I did) but because I felt shoehorned into a role and was frustrated not to be included in other conversations. That situation has definitely changed for the better.

I would be very interested in seeing a comparison, by gender, of how writers are paid. That would be the real test.

There is today an ongoing debate around the word "genre" in the science fiction/horror milieu. Some agree with Ursula K. Le Guin that it is socially prejudiced; others claim that it is an essential and necessary literary "identity." What is your position on the subject?
I've always hated the word "genre"—to me, it's purely a marketing and commercial tool, and one that may finally have lost its utility. Numerous quote-unquote literary writers have been writing "genre" fiction for years, under other names—magical realism, speculative fiction, slipstream, dystopian, whatever—anything to avoid the book being labeled as science fiction. Margaret Atwood (who should have known better) made a point of saying she didn't write science fiction, but speculative fiction. To me, it's all fiction, and should be judged on its own terms. I ignore genre when I'm writing, and I try to ignore it when I'm reviewing. The UK critic John Clute has popularized the extremely useful term "fantastika"[1] (from the Russian), as an umbrella term that covers numerous genres.

You write horror, science fiction, dark fantasy, and "noir." What is determinant in your choice of these genres?
Basically, I have a story to tell and a particular mood I'd like to project, and I decide which mood is most suitable to the story. Often, I choose wrong, and write versions of a novel before I get it right. *Generation Loss* started as a contemporary fantasy novel like

[1] https://sf-encyclopedia.com/entry/fantastika

Waking the Moon, then changed to a horror novel, and finally ended up as noir (with flourishes of fantastika). The basic plot and characters remained the same throughout, but the mood and mode changed. Some with *Wylding Hall*, which started as a YA riff on Du Maurier's *Rebecca* and ended up as something very different.

What writers have you been influenced by ? Were their gender important to you?
Angela Carter, Samuel R. Delany, Ursula Le Guin, John Crowley, Gene Wolfe, Robert Graves, Kelly Link, Robert Aickman, Peter Høeg, Kirsten Ekman, M. John Harrison, Patricia Highsmith.

I came of age as a reader in the 1960s and early 70s. Most of the writers I read and admired were men, because most of the writers getting published at that time were men, so that was my default. Gender didn't seem important, until I discovered Angela Carter at the age of eighteen—she was the first woman writer I read where I thought, *that's* what I want to write. Not that I wanted to imitate her, but up until then I really didn't have any artistic role models. So many of the women writers and artists I read or read about seemed to have troubled lives—Jean Rhys, Isadora Duncan, Sylvia Plath, Dorothy Parker, Zelda Fitzgerald. Colette seemed happy, but she was French! Discovering Patti Smith and Angela Carter within a few months of each other in 1975 made me realize, I can do this, too.

What do you think renders horror genres apt to engage in sexual politics?
Horror is a literature of extremes that allows writers to push beyond the limits of ordinary experience. With dystopian science fiction, one might ask, "What's the worst world I can imagine?" Whereas with horror, I can say, "What's the worst person I can imagine? What's the worst thing that someone could experience?" You can extrapolate answers to these questions, or create fictional scenarios inspired by them, and use them as templates for a story.

The several subcategories that emerged with regard to horror (gay, lesbian, transgender, feminist, black, etc.), enhanced by the different anthologies that we can find in the market, not only signify the portrayal of specific identities or communities, but also each of them seems to address a specific audience. Do you write/with a gendered audience in mind?

Never. I write what I need and want to write, and hope it will find its audience. This can change from book to book, but I think my readers approach my work knowing they'll find a certain dark vision that isn't necessarily connected to any gender (or genre).

Going back to your characters, I noticed that your male figures are usually more fragile and vulnerable than the female ones. You also have a noir series with a tough and complex main character, Cass Neary. Could this be read as a "gender politics" statement?

That's an incredibly interesting question, also one I've never been asked before. But, looking back at my work from the very beginning of my career, it often featured vulnerable men, from Cass Tyrone in "On the Town Route" to my present novel, *Hokuloa Road*. I started to list individual characters by name and novel/story but quickly realized there are too many of them!

I'm not sure I'd characterize all of these male characters as fragile, but they are emotionally open, which makes them vulnerable. And they're often imperiled. I don't see it as a political statement—many of my characters are inspired to varying degrees by people I know, and these men reflect their real-life inspirations. Cass Neary is very much drawn from my own life and experience—in some ways, the books could qualify as what we now call auto-fiction—but she's much tougher than I am. I wasn't thinking, Oh, I'll make her a powerful, unsympathetic, complex, middle-aged, bisexual, female character—I just wrote her as she appeared in my head. Of course, now it looks like I meant to do that, but in 2006, when the book was being shopped around, it was met with enormous pushback from editors who were put off by the very things that have made Cass an enduring character. *The Girl with the Dragon Tattoo* hadn't appeared yet (it came out a year after *Generation Loss*), so there was no template for someone like Cass.

With my forthcoming novel, *Hokuloa Road*, I did make the decision to depict a young male protagonist who would be put in danger. I felt that, if the character were female, readers might spend the entire novel worrying about her safety, whereas a male protagonist traveling alone wouldn't necessarily worry about being the victim of sexual violence. I also made a decision not to show any women being injured, murdered, or violated, and to have any potential victims be both male and female. So that was a conscious decision to try to avoid sexist tropes depicting violence in a crime novel.

CHAPTER EIGHT

Marie Howalt

Marie Howalt (born in 1981) is a Danish science fiction writer. Notable works: *We Lost the Sky* (novel, 2019), *The Stellar Snow Job* (novella, 2022).

Dear Marie Howalt, thank you very much for accepting to answer these few questions. This book is going to focus specifically on the notions of "gender" and "genre". In this light, can you tell us about your background and how this, in your eyes, influenced the person and the writer you are today?
Thank you for having me! It is an honor to be part of this project!

I have always been fascinated with science fiction and fantasy. There was a children's show featuring a giant teddy bear on TV when I was a toddler, and in some episodes, he went to visit another planet. Those captured my attention and imagination right away and were my absolute favorite.

I grew up in Denmark in the 1980s, and I did not have a particularly gendered upbringing, in the sense that I was not told to wear clothing or colors assigned to a specific gender, and I played as much with toy cars and action figures as I did with dolls. I assume that back then, toys were generally not marketed in the gendered way they are now. Toys such as Playmobil and Lego were Playmobil and Lego for everybody. Kids were just kids. I've noticed a certain gender bias in the marketing in later sets, as if girls were more inclined to play with hairdressers and princesses and boys with astronauts and adventurers. But I think the trend may be turning around to more interest-based and not gender-based/biased values.

I watched *Star Wars* and *Star Trek* (reruns of the original series as well as *The Next Generation* and *Deep Space Nine*) in my childhood, and though we can probably all agree that later iterations of both franchises have more inclusive representations and less gender bias, they still showed me that a princess could have as much agency as any male counterpart, that a black person and a white person could be equals, that women could be admirals, and so on.

Of course, I also read all the science fiction and fantasy books I could get my hands on. There was not a lot in the local library, especially not for children and teenagers who, apparently, were expected to primarily read realistic stories that, for the most part, did not feel any more relevant to me than speculative fiction did. And until I learned English, I had to rely on Danish translations.

I was eleven when I decided that if the library could not supply me with enough of the books I wanted to read, I would just write my own stories. When my family got an internet connection in the late 1990s, I got involved in a few fandoms and wrote, before knowing the term existed, some fanfics, but I enjoyed writing about my own worlds and characters more. And I have always wanted to share those worlds and characters with others.

After high school (or the Danish equivalent, gymnasium), I went on to study English and religion at the University of Copenhagen. I focused mostly on literature, and during this time, I learned that a much broader spectrum of speculative fiction existed than what I had previously known. Even though I personally felt that the fantasy genres had merit and were not pure escapism or entertainment, it was the sentiment most people around me had until I began taking courses on various kinds of speculative fiction. I became familiar with the works of, for instance, Jeanette Winterson and Margaret Atwood, and I began to understand, from an academic viewpoint, how speculative fiction can be critical or provide commentary on our society. It can ask questions, examine the human condition, warn, criticize, inspire, and so on, as well as any other kind of literature. I wrote my master's thesis on magic realism and urban fantasy.

Some of my stories have been published online and in short story collections, but my first traditionally published book came out from Spaceboy Books in 2019. Now three more have joined it, and I am working on several books set in the same universe as my latest, a diverse space opera crime/comedy.

Speculative fiction—and science fiction, in particular—has traditionally been regarded as a male-oriented genre. Before the advent of second-wave feminism and the gay liberation movement in the 1960s, women writers were denied recognition not as much by publishing houses as by science fiction nominations and awards. Even today, science fiction is still considered as mainly appealing to men and fantasy as being more welcoming to women. How do you feel about this gender-oriented differentiation among genres in Denmark? Do you feel that it is still present or more a thing of the past?

The bias toward or domination by men is not unique to the speculative genres. Historically, the same can be said for literature in general, as well as a lot of other things. Speculative fiction and especially science fiction, however, seem to have adapted more slowly than certain other literary genres. Perhaps, the idea that science is only relevant to males has lingered for longer than other subjects.

However, I feel that there are two misconceptions inherent in a gender-orientated genre differentiation. First, there is the idea that men enjoy (or should we go as far as to say, "are able to understand"?) reading or writing about technology and science, while women (and other genders, though this discussion is usually put in a binary context) would much rather read and write about magic and romance. I feel this is an outdated assumption at best. Also, if there has been a historical bias against science fiction from a nonmale reader point of view, the objection might not be against science but against women being treated only as victims or romantic interests in older works of science fiction.

Secondly, the whole premise of differentiation, even if we accept the gender difference as valid, is faulty, at least nowadays, because a lot of science fiction does not content itself with hard science, but focuses more on character development, philosophy, or fantastic creatures. And vice versa: fantasy can have very rigid and logical magic systems or concern itself with warfare or other traditionally male-dominated subjects.

One could suggest that contemporary society had to make it acceptable for nonmales to be interested in science before literature could catch up. But generally speaking, it feels absurd to me that a genre like science fiction that literally concerns itself with the future and with new ideas should be stuck in an outdated view of gender and gender roles, when it comes to writers, readers, as well as the content of the works themselves.

In Denmark, fantasy appears to be more popular than science fiction in general. Perhaps that has to do with the mainstream spotlight that fantasy has enjoyed via *The Lord of the Rings* movies and the *Game of Thrones* TV series. I feel that fantasy has thus transcended the idea that it is for a niche audience and became accessible to more people. So, while I can name a lot more Danish female fantasy authors than science fiction authors, I am not convinced it is due to a present-day gender bias rather than to the fact that the genre did not become that popular and therefore did not attract as many new writers of any gender, leaving mostly older, and thus mostly male, authors on the scene.

Do you think women in horror and science fiction are in a better position today than when you began to write? Do you feel any gendered resistance in the milieu or in the reviews?
I find that the speculative genres are and have been evolving for a long time. As they should. We see an increasing number of writers of color, queer writers, and female writers being published. I know there has been some backlash against this development in certain parts of the community, and as far as I can tell, it largely has to do with the idea that the inclusion of a more diverse cluster of writers is somehow fad or it means exclusion of the rest (i.e., white male). I find it hard to share this concern. The way I see it, it is now simply becoming possible, though not necessarily easy, for writers to be published regardless of ethnicity, skin color, or gender. This is also reflected in more diversity within literature itself.

On a personal level, I do not think I have been subject to much gender bias as a writer. My first traditionally published book only came out in 2019, however, and I do imagine that the tale would have been quite different, if I had tried to get published earlier.

Sometimes, I run into people outside of the publishing world who are surprised that I write science fiction because I do not fit in their (now slightly outmoded) idea of what a science fiction writer should be.

Did you encounter any discrimination specifically related to gender in your writing career?
I have been fortunate so far when it comes to avoiding gender discrimination. I hope it is a sign that the industry is changing. I do encounter an emphasis on "women writers" or "queer writers"

from time to time, however. I can completely understand why it is necessary to point to these aspects, given that the publishing industry still has a certain bias, but I hope we will reach a point when writers can just be writers one day.

There is today an ongoing debate around the word "genre" in the science fiction/horror milieu. Some agree with Ursula K. Le Guin that it is socially prejudiced; others claim that it is an essential and necessary literary "identity." What is your position on the subject?
The debate about genre is relevant, but it is also a very difficult issue.

On the one hand, it is necessary to label books somehow because there are a lot of works out there. People want to know what sort of book they are picking up—if it is going to be a scary read, or one with spaceships in it, or one about a dystopian society, and so on. To that end, genre is an easy way to identify a work. And the more specified the genre term is (e.g., psychological horror or solarpunk science fiction), the easier.

On the other hand, I completely agree that there is a prejudice against the so-called genre fiction. An idea that it is pulp, pure entertainment without any literary merit or relevance.

When I began to publish my novels online a decade ago, I was very reluctant to attribute a genre label to them. I would sometimes describe them as "fantasy with a literary twist" or something to that effect in an attempt to convey that what I wrote aspired to be more than what I imagined readers would expect from a given speculative fiction work. In hindsight, I think there is the same risk of accidentally enforcing the prejudice by hinting that "this one is not like *other* books in the genre," as there is of inadvertently implying that women are normally weak by using the term "strong female protagonist." That is not to say that I do not understand why it can be necessary to use this term, especially if female characters with agency are under-represented in a certain genre. But it can accidentally strengthen the stereotype that it is trying to break.

As mentioned before, I think science fiction has been a bit slow to embrace diversity—in writers, characters, and generally in terms of what is acceptable within the genre. Nowadays, I have grown to embrace genre labels more. This is at least partly due to the development within the genres. My books would not fit in a pool consisting of 1950s or 60s science fiction. But I am proud to be in the company of Yoon Ha Lee, Becky Chambers, Hugh Howey, and so on.

Now that science fiction encompasses this wider scope, I would rather label my books as science fiction and take part in defining what this genre can be today than enhancing the stereotype by calling them something else. I suppose, in a way, I am arguing for reclaiming the genre names and moving them beyond prejudice.

What was determinant in your choice of the genre you have chosen to write with?
In general, I write stories about people, about universal themes, and the experience of being human. These stories primarily end up as speculative fiction for me, and I have dabbled in alternative history, urban fantasy, and a tiny bit of horror. But these days, I mostly write various kinds of science fiction. It is a genre I have always enjoyed reading and which has a lot of potential, in my opinion. I do like to mix genres a bit, however, and to add aspects that may not be prevalent in my chosen genre.

While I am not going to pretend that I do not think of genre at all, I will say that for me, the characters, the general mood of the story, and a plot idea come first. I have those little puzzle pieces, and in assembling them, I find out what genre lends itself best to the story I want to tell. And that said, it is probably not a coincidence that I end up with science fiction these days. I find that this genre fits the questions and themes that I want to explore very well.

The 1960s and 70s are perhaps the most influential decades in the study of gender in speculative fiction. Not only was there an influx of female speculative fiction writers, but also many of these writers applied feminist theory to speculative fiction (Ursula K. Le Guin, Angela Carter, etc.). At the same time, the emergence of African-American female voices brought to light the intersectionality between gender and race. It is as if speculative fiction genres offered better than others the opportunity to challenge social conventions, especially gender, and to explore alternative sexualities and alliances. Is it the case in your work? Have you been influenced by specific writers of this generation?
I strongly believe that the speculative genres are suitable to comment on or challenge the conventions of our society. Any literature can do that, of course, but if we take science fiction as an example, it is possible to create any kind of variation of our society and expose it by taking it to the extreme. Or, create something entirely new based

on ideals or fears. I would venture so far as to say that providing this kind of juxtaposition is one of science fiction's finest purposes. I consider my own works at the subtler, more modest end of that scale, but it is without a doubt an element that is present.

As much as I enjoy Ursula K. Le Guin's works, I came to them a little late in my own journey as a writer, by which I mean during or after the end of my university studies. The same goes for Octavia E. Butler. That does not mean I cannot be influenced by them, but they were not part of my early formative years, so to speak.

Margaret Atwood, however, was part of those years for me. Most of her speculative works were published a little later, but they are all still prime examples of this kind of commentary. She and Jeanette Winterson were the writers that made a much younger me realize just how extremely relevant and important speculative fiction can be.

I think there is a second wave of the same kind happening right now. The doors have been wedged open by the earlier generation for writers of color, female and queer writers alike. And now, it seems to me, there is a revolution coming from within the speculative genres. Among the important voices of this redefinition of science fiction (which is the speculative genre I am most up to date with), I would mention Yoon Ha Lee, Becky Chambers, N. K. Jemisin, Nicky Drayden, Kameron Hurley, Ann Leckie, Annalee Newitz, and Mary Robinette Kowal. They all tackle issues like gender, race, and sexuality, though in very different ways.

We also find writers like Lois McMaster Bujold and Martha Wells in this category, but their writing careers span over a longer period, and that makes them an interesting study in a slightly different way. It is fascinating to see the way they have been able to challenge the boundaries of the speculative genres from within decades. It seems to me that they were under restraints and limited by the (male-dominated) conventions of the genres when they were first published, but what was suggested between the lines in their early works is now fully out in the open.

On your Instagram profile, you present yourself as an author of "casually queer" science fiction. Could you say precisely what you mean by this?
When I call my books casually queer, I am attempting to convey that they feature queer characters in leading roles, but also that the fact that they are queer is not a main focus or, perhaps more

accurately, not a problematic thing within the context of the stories. So far, my books have not been coming-out stories or stories focusing on characters struggling or coming to terms with their gender identities or sexual orientations (which does not mean that I do not think there is a need for those stories). Or, put in another way, the characters just happen to be queer, like they happen to be spaceship pilots, or AI engineers, or nomads, or what have you. Queerness is part of them and part of the society they live in and not a main defining feature. My books tend to take place in a diverse space where gender, ethnicity, and sexuality are, on the whole, not presented as problematic.

What in your eyes renders speculative fiction apt to engage in sexual politics?
Literature does not exist in a void. It is always written and published in a context, whether intentionally political or not.

This is true for any kind of literature, but I find that speculative fiction is an especially fantastic tool to engage in a modern discourse. It can be intended to maintain a status quo or to create a new world order. The goal of a lot of science fiction in particular, I feel, is to influence the future in one way or another. A dystopian novel, for instance, will always be about breaking the system, or at least breaking out of it.

But I think one of the beauties of speculative fiction is that it can also treat a large variety of subjects in very subtle ways. Sexual politics can be presented in the shape of a pansexual elven community in a fantasy novel, or a future in which physically transitioning from a person's birth-assigned gender is an instant and easy thing for them to do. A good example is Mary Robinette Kowal's *The Spare Man*, which is a witty detective story set on a cruise ship in space. Apart from treating mental and physical disabilities in a respectful and authentic way, every character introduces themself by name and pronoun (in her own words, from a TikTok video, "If you are writing science fiction and your future has a binary gender structure, you are doing it wrong.") It is a wonderfully simple way of showing diversity.

How is this genre modified in order to accommodate contemporary post-identitarian claims in your novels? How do you manage to negotiate this tension between tradition and new sexuality-related topics with respect to gender images?

It is strange to me when a work of science fiction is essentially only a picture of how the world looks right now with a few robots or spaceships thrown into the mix. Science fiction is excellent at challenging our past, our present, and our possible future. When I write about an imagined future, it is natural for me to describe societies that grow out of the world I live in now. My books are not about what I think will happen in the future in a 1:1 sense, but they are my takes on how people individually or as a society might react when faced with a given situation. And they grapple with some universal challenges to humanity.

One example of how I try to navigate between various worldviews is the relationship between the four major societies or ways of living in *the Moonless trilogy*. The social structures of the city of Florence are based on what feels old-fashioned to a contemporary person in regards to its view on, for instance, gender and sexuality. The wanderers can be read as archaic in a technological sense, but a lot of their views align with contemporary society. The long-gone past society in the books is essentially a sketch of our future in which some things have changed a lot, and others have not. Finally, a new society emerges, and it attempts to be egalitarian while holding on to certain aspects from each of the others, which, of course, is harder to do than to talk about.

The several subcategories that emerged with regard to speculative fiction (gay, lesbian, transgender, feminist, black, etc.), enhanced by the different anthologies that we can find in the market, not only signify the portrayal of specific identities or communities, but also each of them seems to address a specific audience. Do you write with a gendered audience in mind?
It would be wrong to say that I do not have an idea of my target audience(s), in general and with the variation that inevitably comes from writing books of different (sub)genres. However, I do not write with a gendered audience in mind as my only possible readers. Nor with one of a specific political or religious conviction, nor any particular ethnicity or culture.

I hope to give queer people and other minorities or traditionally marginalized groups adventures where they see characters like themselves in an unproblematic way and with as much agency and variation as historically has only been given to specific groups. I want them to be able to think, "Oh, people like me can be protagonists too. People like me can be valid fiction characters."

But I also want other social and sexual groups to be able to enjoy them. I want them to be able to think, "Oh, this sort of space adventure that I like can have a queer protagonist who is as real and multifaceted as everyone else!"

I would like my books to be approachable to a lot of different people. Some readers might put more emphasis on a given part of the reading experience than others, but that is how it should be. I hope that my books can bring up certain subjects and allow readers to form their own opinions.

Do you think that speculative fiction works are differently structured when addressed to traditionally under-portrayed individuals or communities?
Generally, I think it is more a question of the sender than the receiver, so to speak. When someone is writing from their own perspective or culture, that will inevitably structure the book in some way. Everybody has their own frame of reference, but, of course, writers also spend a great deal of time widening that frame.

All books are written by a person and within a society. When I pick up Chinese science fiction or Afrofuturism, for example, I can often feel that I lack in my intuitive understanding of the culture that a particular work has grown out of. As a reader, I welcome the opportunity to learn something new.

So, thinking of it like that, I imagine that if, for instance, someone is not used to thinking in nonbinary terms, they will have to get used to the language in a book with nonbinary characters. Perhaps it makes sense to say that everyone who is not used to a given language or structure has to put in a little bit more work to get the most out of the reading experience.

That said, every book has a target audience, and as a writer, you will need to know what kind of audience you speak to. You will need to decide whether you want to explain certain things or not. And I believe that speculative fiction writers are well equipped to do that.

Is the portrayal of a minority specifically addressed to those that feel portrayed in these works?
There are undoubtedly books which are addressed to specific minorities, but I do not believe all books have to be. I think of my

own books as double-edged swords in that respect; I want those groups to feel seen and safe and I want to open people's eyes to a new way of looking at things. Both are examples of how I feel science fiction aspires to change the world, even if just a little.

It always makes me happy when readers feel seen and accepted in my books, whether they are queer, disabled, of an ethnic minority, and so on. One reader recently told me how happy it made them to read in *The Stellar Snow Job* about a character with a disability similar to theirs who had agency and was treated respectfully in the book. Others have pointed out similar things with regard to gender and sexuality. And, I really want to give readers that safe space, where these aspects of the characters are just what they are and are not treated as problematic in what I write.

But I am also very happy when readers who do not belong to a traditionally marginalized group feel they get something more out of my books than entertainment alone. I remember that when the first *Moonless* book came out, several readers told me the use of gender-neutral pronouns used for sentient androids made them stop and think about the way a lot of things are gendered and assigned stereotypical or outdated values.

In your *Moonless Trilogy* (*We Lost the Sky*, *Seeking Shelter*, *Heart of the Storm*), you create a postapocalyptic world in which different types of societies live side by side: a centralized city, nomads, and an anarchist-inspired community. In many ways, it feels like a positive version of Ursula Le Guin's more pessimistic take on politics, as in *The Dispossessed*. Would you consider your trilogy as part of the "solarpunk" movement? How political do you consider your writing to be?

I think most people confuse postapocalyptic fiction with dystopia and a bleak view of the world. And very often, this is the case. There is a sense of "Look, this is how bad things can get" feeling to those stories. Whether it is a manmade disaster that destroyed our way of life or something else, there is a foreboding or warning quality to them.

Moonless is a complicated matter. The books follow four different kinds of societies, in a way. One of them does not exist anymore in the books, but there are a lot of remnants from it, such as a couple of protagonists and a lot of semi-forgotten technology. The other three are the nomad community, the sheltered city, and the new society that some of the main characters struggle to build. All of them have good sides and bad sides. Granted, it is easier to sympathize with some than with others, but there are people doing their best in all of them. And they all have doubtful aspects. Nothing, especially not of the magnitude of a society, is simple. I hope to show that with my books. The new community is a melting pot of sorts that welcomes people from everywhere else. It is the characters' earnest attempt to create something sustainable, in several senses of that word. The new society in *Moonless* is just one way to do it, the way that makes sense for the characters in that world. It is not a template.

With all that said, however, I believe that literature is more about asking the right questions than imposing a set of fixed answers on the reader. Asking questions and brainstorming ideas about the consequences is one of the purposes of speculative fiction, in my view.

I did not intend for *Moonless* to be solarpunk when I began to write it. I do not think I had even heard of that term, when I came up with the initial idea. But I like refreshing takes on genres and mixing genres. And I have described *Moonless* before as "optimistic postapocalyptic fiction". If solarpunk in general is concerned with an inclusive society, and with sustainable energy, then the books certainly have solarpunk elements.

I generally do not write with the intention for my books to be primarily political, but I think they do have an experimental and maybe even a universal political message.

Gender preoccupation is also very present in your writing, both in the *Moonless Trilogy* and your new science fiction detective novella, *The Stellar Snow Job*. Some of your characters are queer; some are gay, bisexual, or pansexual, others nonbinary; and finally some are "straight." And, as in Le Guin's *Earthsea* series, most of them are nonwhites. Do you see this as a prediction or as a statement on our Western society?

My stories are most often about flawed people trying their best. In the *Moonless* books, it made sense to me that a group of diverse people breaking away from other communities and trying to establish their own, based on their ideals and their experiences, would strive to make the new one respectful and inclusive.

In the *Colibri Investigations* books, humans have joined an established Union of sentient species across the galaxy. A lot of these species have had centuries or even millennia longer than humanity to make mistakes and try to do better, and they have each other to point out what parts of their societies are broken. So, the Union has rules and laws that they impose on humanity, so that we have to rise to the occasion. But not all these rules and demands align with the people in the books (or the people who read them). At the same time, suddenly being just one species out of many, having to play by certain interstellar rules, makes humans reconsider a lot of their ways. It is easier to unite when you have a common . . . well, not enemy, but outside relation.

I like to think of my books as inclusive when it comes to queerness, ethnicity, and so on. They are not necessarily predictions or statements. In my view, some of the societies in my books do have some very good things going on for them, but they are not recipes.

All sexual orientations are seen as acceptable in your novels, and there is no sexual prejudice present in either the dialogues or the situations. Do you feel that the genre makes your message available to a larger audience?
When a story is set in the future or in a different world altogether, a writer has to choose what elements to bring with them from the present and the past of the world they and their readers live in. As a writer, you have to consider which discourses you want to speak in and how you want to do it. Do you want to magnify a real issue to show how badly you think it can end? Do you want to show your version of an ideal society? Or do you want to write about a world that is essentially structured like the one you live in now with fantastical elements thrown in to explore how we would deal with something like that? And, of course, how clear do you want to make your own view?

Speculative fiction is a great vessel for presenting various takes on society and people in general. And yes, in a way, it probably does make the deeper contents, whatever they may be, more readily available to a larger audience. But then again, the speculative genres are, as mentioned earlier, also still dismissed by some people.

In the futures I write about, people have largely moved on from a lot of the concerns we find in our contemporary society because those settings fit the stories I want to tell.

In the *Moonless* books, the domed city has been secluded from the rest of the world for centuries, and the ruling class seeks to uphold a social status quo that they find desirable. In that city, there is a lack of acceptance for people who live outside the norms. You will not find any women in power or any openly gay characters as long as they live there. But in the other communities, new and old, no one is stigmatized because of gender or sexuality.

In the *The Stellar Snow Job* (and the following *Colibri Investigations* books), having recently become part of an interstellar Union, humanity has moved away from its internal issues. There are simply bigger things to deal with than what is in someone's trousers and with whom, if any, they prefer to be intimate. It is a world that has moved on from some of the questions that are prevalent in our contemporary society.

CHAPTER NINE

Ai Jiang

Ai Jiang (born in 1997) is a Chinese-born Canadian science fiction, horror, and fantasy writer. Notable works: *Linghun* (novella, 2023).

Dear Ai Jiang, many thanks for accepting to be part of this volume, which will focus specifically on the notions of "gender" and "genre." In this light, can you tell us about your background and how this, in your eyes, influenced the person and the writer you are today?

My background, I'd say, is complicated—albeit not as complicated as some but more complicated than others—and I think being in Canada has been further complicating my identity, as I age and as society and culture are rapidly changing around me. I was born in Changle, Fujian Province, and oscillated between relatives on my father's side in a village in Shanghu and my mother's side in Changle, though I spent more time with my grandparents on my mother's side back in China after my parents immigrated to Canada first before bringing me over when I was four. And, because it's customary for my grandmother's traditions to have the parents live with their sons if they have any, my father's mother lives with us rather than my aunts.

Until I entered high school, my grandmother was the one taking care of my sister and I most of the time while my parents worked— sometimes multiple jobs, so a lot of my upbringing was quite traditional but it was also infused with what I was exposed to at school. The values and beliefs shared by my grandmother and my parents did not always align with what we were taught at school or experienced in society. This gap is greater now eith the rapid. In comparison—because of my childhood and how it differs from my sister's, who was born in Canada—I often have questions about my values, beliefs, and identity and how to reconcile them with Canadian society's and my family's.

One particular aspect is the emphasis placed on boys and men. Particularly on my father's side of the family, a firm belief is that sons are far more valuable than daughters: they must be the breadwinners of the family; they must be strong and stoic, a mountain or stone or anchor for the family; whereas for women, they're to be the homemakers, the childbearers, the ones who aren't expected to have high education or high-paying jobs.

And, I think my background has shaped both what I write and the direction I want to take my work in, where I want to better understand my culture but also subvert its long-standing beliefs. I've been both passive and resistant to the gender expectations and traditions of my culture, always having to choose my battles carefully as well as the timing of them, and knowing which are the ones I can win and which might be lost on my change-resistant family.

I would say that my family has come a long way already, looking back to when we first arrived, but the change is slow. My parents are far more open now, and my grandmother, though still quite stubborn, has been more accepting of things differing greatly from when she was my age. But I think this desire for change and the resistance to it is something I explore often as a writer and would like to continue to explore, hoping to create more open-minded and inclusive work.

Do you feel any gendered resistance or stigmatization in the milieu or in the reviews?
In the writing community, I feel I've been very fortunate to not have experienced any gendered resistance or stigmatization— though it is only for those I have worked with, spoken with, or connected with, and there might be other corners of the community that might be far more vicious than what i can imagine. There may always be both conscious and unconscious gender resistance or stigmatization, but I often give the benefit of the doubt rather than believing someone might be intentionally malicious or excluding.

Did you encounter any discrimination specifically related to your gender in your writing career?
I have yet to experience discrimination specifically related to my gender in my writing career in terms of the writing community, though I have with my family. But I suppose with my family it was more of a matter of being able to make a living. I have had an aunt who told me it was a woman's role to tend to the house and have the children and that I shouldn't worry too much about having a career.

There is an ongoing debate about the word "genre" in the science fiction/horror milieu. Some agree with Ursula K. Le Guin that it is socially prejudiced; others claim it is an essential and necessary literary "identity." As you have chosen to write a novella and stories which use the tropes of ghost stories, science fiction, and fantasy, what is your position on the subject?
I think the lines between genres and what is considered "genre" and "literary" are becoming more blurred. Prejudiced ways of thinking about "genre" in the past, though still prevalent, hold far less weight now. For me, because I've read mostly "literary classics" throughout my life, my writing style, motivation, and intentions within my horror, science fiction, and fantasy stories are informed by the "literary" and take on its tones. I think horror, science fiction, fantasy, and all their subgenres have the ability to complexify subvert social and political conventions, and explore complex emotions and relationship dynamics as much as realist works without elements of the speculative or the fantastic.

What was the determinant factor in your choice of these genres?
Horror, science fiction, fantasy, and its subgenres allow me to be more receptive to exploring ideas that might not be present in current society or dig further into humanity and our world's culture and politics from new angles. Through the metaphorical, I can reevaluate my current beliefs and values and better understand those of others. These genres allow me to envision better worlds, more dystopian worlds, and examine aspects of our own world with greater flexibility.

What writers have you been influenced by? Was their gender important to you?
Given my background in English Literature, a lot of what I read in school were older classics with reading lists that weren't particularly

diverse, though some courses more than others tried to include a greater range of voices, and I took those courses when I could.

Writers who have influenced me include Toni Morrison, Kazuo Ishiguro, Ken Liu, Ted Chiang, Shirley Jackson, Bram Stoker, Virginia Woolf, Don DeLillo, Margaret Atwood, Ursula K. Le Guin, Xiran Jay Zhao, Zadie Smith, Hayao Miyazaki, Ruth Ozeki, Jhumpa Lahiri, Octavia E. Butler, among others.

The gender of these writers wasn't important to me, more so the writing and the stories they were trying to tell, the uniqueness of their voices and perspectives, and their experiences. Though these elements are all affected by things such as the class, race, gender, and sexuality of the writers, I wanted to read a wide variety of voices. I'm still working on stretching myself further in my reading, to be more conscious about what I read and who the works are written by. I think particularly in the current cultural and political landscape, being intentional with our reading is becoming a very important thing—which voices we choose to amplify, to support, to encourage to speak further and louder. Taste in writing style is still very much subjective, but having an openness to trying new works and accepting new voices, I believe, is a choice.

What do you think renders horror genres apt to engage in identity and sexual politics?
I find that oftentimes horror is very introspective, allowing writers to dig deep into their psyches and explore emotional and identity truths (not always of course!). But especially with horror subgenres like body horror and psychological horror, I feel that these are conductive to engage in identity and sexual politics—how our thoughts manifest in our minds, how they might evolve and change, or how our bodies may feel foreign, unbelonging to ourselves or controlled, and agency dictated by others.

Do you write with a gendered audience in mind?
I write with a general audience in mind—usually an adult audience rather than young adults or children. I often try to reconcile the cultural elements of my work with that of Western story standards and expectations for literature hoping to reach a wider readership. Emotional connection to a broad public is what I often attempt for my work.

Do you think that horror and fantasy works are differently structured when addressed to traditionally under-portrayed individuals or communities?

I don't think they are structured differently to address traditionally under-portrayed individuals or communities, but I do think an individual's background, culture, and experiences might shape the stories and inform the way they are told, which can mean that it might differ from how stories are told by the dominant culture or how they have been told throughout literary traditions in the past.

Would you say that the portrayal of a minority is specifically addressed to those that feel portrayed in these works?

Yes and no. I think it depends on the intention of the author's work. Some might target their writing specifically to those the work portrays, hoping these communities and groups might see a representation of themselves. But others might write to amplify the voices of their communities and for them to become more common in publishing and writing markets. Or, perhaps, a mixture of both.

Your novella *Linghun* is a ghost story about a mysterious town, called HOME, where families live with the ghost of one of their members. Although it is a multicultural town, and the main characters are of different ethnicities, there is a strong Chinese cultural feeling pervading the story. Did you want to work with a cultural specificity attached to Chinese traditions, or did you have a larger aim? In other words, did you feel that the ghost-story genre offered you a possibility for a transnational narrative, as these types of stories exist all over the world?

Originally, I had the novella focus more on mortality, humanity, and how humans deal with the loss of a loved one and how they might mourn the dead. I didn't intend for it to have a cultural specificity attached to Chinese traditions, because the many ways of mourning depicted within the novella are not based on specific traditions. However, the characters' backgrounds inform their experiences, which draws a connection between Wenqi and Mrs., both emphasizing the parallel in their experiences but also works to juxtapose them. There is a sense of the loss of home, the loss of time, the loss of one's culture, which is something I believe many can connect with, whether or not they might be from Chinese culture. I think ghost stories in this sense offer a transnational narrative. We all mourn the dead, we all wish to turn back time, and we all have lost someone we have loved, and still do love—and sometimes that someone is ourselves, and sometimes that someone is still alive.

As a writer with a Chinese background, a Canadian education, and having studied abroad for a year in Scotland, do you feel that gender borders exist?

I think gender borders exist no matter where I might be in the world, but more so in some places compared to others. I have noticed instances where people might find me much more approachable because I'm female, or perceive that I am weaker for the same reason. Men of my culture—many, not all—might treat me like I'm fragile, dainty, dependent, and maybe sometimes I am, but that doesn't mean these are the only things I can be; and it doesn't mean that men cannot be these things, too.

In some of your stories, such as "Earthquakes Are Coming" and "Fisheyes," family plays an important role in the narratives. Do you feel that it is a condition of the genre of horror itself (since the birth of gothic) or do you want to express something about gender roles through the traditional tropes?

I think for these stories, in particular, I wanted to highlight the bonds between family and the strength of it in facing our horrors and fear ("The Earthquakes Are Coming"); but also, the failure of family and a lack of connection as our greatest fear ("Fisheyes"). In "Xiǎo Èmó—Little Demon," I explore the gender roles of historical China and how women are forced to be submissive childbearers. It's something that has improved, but a mindset that I would say still exists. Similarly, in "The Catcher in the Eye" and "Missing Dolls Around the World," I explore similar issues concerning gender roles—the expectation and presentation of women, their objectification, in society, as well as men and their "duties" and toxic masculinity.

As a reader with a Chinese background, do you feel differences in the ways genders are tackled in Western and Asian genre literature? If yes, how does this influence your own writing?

I think in Asian genre literature, comparatively to Western genre literature, women and their roles may be far more passive overall.

Women are often depicted as a support for the male characters or as secondary characters with little depth. There is a great focus on their appearance and femininity, elegance and docility. But I think this pattern is changing as many writers of Asian descent have been introducing works featuring active female characters, along with nonbinary characters and more passive male characters. It has definitely influenced the direction of my writing in challenging the gender roles that have been ingrained into me while growing up— the same gender roles I have been finding myself resisting more and more with each passing day.

CHAPTER TEN

Penny Jones

Penny Jones (born in 1980) is a British horror writer. Notable works: *Suffer Little Children* (collection, 2019), *Matryochka* (novella, 2021).

Dear Penny Jones, thank you very much for accepting to be part of this volume, which will focus specifically on the notions of "gender" and "genre." In this light, can you tell us about your background and how this, in your eyes, influenced the person and the writer you are today?
I was very lucky that I was brought up by a family that loved to read and who nurtured my passion for stories very early on. My brother is quite a bit older than me and, due to dyslexia, he learnt to read a little later than other children, and when he did, he wanted to share his love of reading with me. So, even before I started school I had already been taught how to read and had been shown the joy that reading can instill in people. My parents also nurtured this passion and, as a three-year-old, I excitedly unwrapped my Christmas presents that consisted of books and a typewriter.

As I grew older, I was equally as lucky that my schools, friends, and family supported me in writing. I also never had that snobbery of why do you want to read/write horror. I was allowed to watch and read pretty much anything I wanted to, though my parents did try and stop me from reading their Pan Books of Horror as they thought them too disturbing for a seven-year-old (this didn't work, I just read them by the bathroom light at two in the morning), and they also told me I needed to be older to watch Stephen Gallagher's

Chimera and to read Mary Shelley's *Frankenstein* as they thought I would struggle to separate the scientific possibilities from the fictional horror elements of the story. This resulted in me watching films such as *Nightmare on Elm Street* and reading Stephen King books, before I ever even glanced at *Frankenstein*.

Although very supportive, my parents wanted me to get a job with regular hours, rather than focus purely on my writing. I did for a while debate going into journalism, but it wasn't where my passion for writing laid. At the time, I had a part-time job as a care assistant alongside going to school. I enjoyed it and was tempted to continue doing that, but my mother pushed me to go for my nursing qualifications. When I applied, the only spaces left were in mental health nursing and I jumped at the chance. In hindsight, I'm really glad that my mother pushed me into going to university, the whole experience and my work as both a mental health nurse and as a general nurse has given me so much more insight into human nature, and both the horrors and joys that people have to deal with in their lives.

What do you think of the position of women in horror today? Do you feel or have you felt any gendered resistance in the milieu or in the reviews?
I see the social media posts and discussions around this all the time, the shares of contents page listings with none or only a token woman gracing their pages, but it isn't something I have noticed having a direct effect on myself. I'm not sure if it's a geographical thing, but certainly the British horror scene seems very supportive of women. I only started to write again as an adult in 2015 and it wasn't long before other writers started suggesting I send my work to calls and small presses that they knew were looking to widen the diversity of their authorship. I'm lucky now to have a really supportive network of both readers and writers, and even luckier to count a lot of those people as friends. I still count myself as a new writer, and I'm lucky if my books get a handful of reviews and recommendations, but I'd say it was pretty much a 50:50 split on those reviews being from male or female readers.

Did you encounter any discrimination specifically related to your gender in your writing career?
Again, I've been lucky and if this has occurred it isn't something I have realized which I find quite surprising, as certainly in my longer

works I tend to have female protagonists, and the horrors that they face are often focused around things, such as pregnancy, parenthood, and their societal relationships.

I wouldn't say that this was discrimination, but there are times when male readers will query aspects of my female characters' behaviors (this is usually prior to publication, so is solicited feedback) and they will often think that the characters' threat response is an overreaction, though the female readers never pick this up as an issue. As a writer and a woman, it is interesting to see how the male/female dynamic responds to perceived danger so differently in our society; that a behavior in a book may be seen as realistic by female readers and fantastical by the male ones. I have thought about toning these reactions down, but I feel it would be doing a disservice to the stories, and that it is important that people realize that these reactions are normal and are not hysterical breakdowns over nonexistent threats.

There is today an ongoing debate around the word "genre" in the science fiction/horror milieu. Some agree with Ursula K. Le Guin that it is socially prejudiced; others claim that it is an essential and necessary literary "identity." What is your position on the subject?
I read for pleasure, it has always been a hobby for me, rather than a way to better myself, and although the majority of the books I read are horror, I also love other genres, as well as literary, contemporary, and classic books. It may be because I could already read by the time I went to school or it might be that I was just lucky with my teachers, but no one has ever disparaged my choice in reading material or the topics that I write about. Actually, thinking back to the books we covered in English classes in school and college, we did *Jane Eyre*, *Great Expectations*, and *Frankenstein* alongside Shakespeare and Wilfred Owen. My teachers always delighted in telling us that these "classics" had been the gothic pulp fictions of their day.

I think that the label "horror" can be helpful to those who are just discovering the genre, but even that loses its usefulness pretty quickly. There are far more horrific occurrences in *Geek Love* by Katherine Dunn than there are in *The Girl who loved Tom Gordon* by Stephen King, but only the latter is found in the horror section of the bookstore.

You write horror. What were the determinant factors in your choice of this genre?

Horror encompasses so many styles and types from the uncanny and quiet, to splatterpunk and extreme horror, but the one thing I feel they all have in common is that they focus on the character. We have to feel for the protagonist to be scared for them; we want a reason to root for them, to fear for them, to be broken by them. Even when my writing strays out of what some people would term as horror, that central facet of trying to get the reader to empathize with the characters is my main aim.

What writers have you been influenced by? Was their gender important to you?

Growing up, my three main influences would have been Shirley Jackson, Stephen King, and John Wyndham. These were authors that family and friends lent me their well-read copies of books, because they knew I'd love them, and they were right. Their gender wasn't important to me then, what was important was something in their writing that spoke to me. For Shirley Jackson, it is the lyrical almost dreamlike telling of her stories. For Stephen King, it is his portrayal of relationships between his characters and his ability to make you care for them and fear them, sometimes in equal measure. Strangely, for John Wyndham, it is his ability to write female protagonists. Wyndham's books were probably the first stories I read where the women weren't shown as being flighty or silly. Prior to reading his works, any female character I had read had either been an air-head bimbo, or if intelligent, they were either too physically weak or too emotionally weak to act on what they knew. Suddenly, with Josella (*The Day of the Triffids*), Ferrelyn (*The Midwich Cuckoos*), and Diana (*Trouble with Lichen*), I had female characters that I felt I could connect with.

As an adult I have tried to expand my reading influences, though this is difficult if you just go along to the bookstore. Every year I chose a different letter of the alphabet and I only read authors whose surnames started with this letter. After this I spent a year only reading authors from countries I hadn't read an author from. Even now before I leave for holidays, I try to pick up a book by an author from the country I am going to—most of these are in translation (but my Danish book is written in Danish and is taking me a while to translate).

Attending writing conventions is also a great way to find new authors. Panels and readings can give you a great insight into styles and topics that different authors specialize in. Modern authors that I love are Robert Shearman and Cate Gardener for their use of the uncanny in their fiction. Alison Moore, **Priya Sharma**, and Tracy Fahey are all wonderful at weaving their lyrical storytelling with much darker undertones that can make you feel really uneasy. Laura Mauro has a heartbreaking strength to her stories. She manages to integrate class system and injustice into her works without ever coming across as preachy or detracting from the tale.

In your opinion, what renders horror genres apt to engage in sexual politics?
I haven't answered this, as I'm not sure about what you mean. Do you mean . . . around such issues as abortion rights, or do you mean feminism, misogyny, etc.? Let me know if you want me to answer this. You may already have enough information from my other answers anyway.

In horror fiction, like many other formulaic genres, characters and situations are very often based on conscious or subconscious stereotypes. How do you manage to negotiate this tension with respect to gender images?
As readers, we like familiarity, we like to be able to see something of ourselves in a character so we can empathize with their story; as a writer, I like to try and surprise or unnerve my reader. Every writer wants a new idea, a new monster, a new plot; though, as they say, there are no new stories. I personally try to balance this by using familiar tropes and everyday horrors in my stories. Every parent knows the fear of looking up from their phone at a playground and their child not being there, everyone knows the anxiety of walking down a dark street late at night, or having the school bullies waiting for you to be on your own. But what I then try to do is to make the characters as nonstereotypical as possible. If I can't tell a new story, at least I can make you care about the people having to live through it by making them as realistic as possible.

Do you write with a gendered audience in mind?
No. I don't have an ideal reader. As a writer, what I want is for everyone to read my work and to love it. And although I know that

this isn't going to happen, I find it very difficult to change my writing to suit others. I find that each story I write has a slightly different voice anyway, and that I tend to write in the style in which the story needs to be told. I have a novel sitting in my drawer which was my attempt at writing a "commercial" book, and all the feedback I got from agents was that they liked it, but it isn't commercial enough. Someday, I'm going to go back and write that novel as the story it wanted to be, rather than the one I thought it should be.

Do you see yourself as a "woman" writer? A "genre" writer? Both or none of those?
I would definitely say I am a horror writer. I love horror and feel really proud to write it and to champion it to others, though I wouldn't take offense if I was referred to under other terms. For me, I want people to realize that horror isn't just torture or stuffy ghost stories; if you tell me what kind of books you enjoy reading, you can bet I'll have a horror book recommendation for you.

In your short stories and novellas, the family structure is a recurrent theme. In "Matryoshka," for example, motherhood is the trigger of the horror in your story. Although male writers have tackled the same subject, sometimes with a different angle, such as Ira Levin in *Rosemary's Baby*, would you say that women writers are more particularly apt at tackling maternity and its issues?
I wouldn't say that women are more apt at tackling maternity in horror, but I do think it is true that male and female writers tend to approach this subject from different angles. In my work, I look at the horror of pregnancy and motherhood being invasive, almost parasitic. There is the physical pain and body transformation that occurs within pregnancy, but there is also that loss of the self, of autonomy; you stop being seen purely as yourself, you are now the vessel of another person. I tend to find that this loss of the self occurs a lot throughout my writing. However, I find that men focus on the horror of the unknown, the child not yet born. The horror is what is yet to come, the tumult and alienness of a newborn, the impact that unknown figures will have on their world. It is an external force rather than an internal pressure.

Childhood and dangerous children are also a trope you use quite often. Is that a statement from your side, as a woman writer, or are

you only using classic tropes, like the siblings in Henry James's *The Turn of the Screw?*

"Write what you know" is a saying that is often bandied about when talking about fiction, and although that can be very boring, I think if you are very truthful about what you know, then it can lead to some very direct works. As a horror writer, it is probably more accurate for me to say "Write what scares you," and children scare me. I find there is an uncanny valley aspect about children; it's probably down to the fact that I don't have a maternal bone in my body, but I find them very alien. There is a dangerous unpredictability within a child; they're still learning right from wrong, and with them being almost purely driven by their *Id* that can lead to some terrifying behaviors. I think back to the pranks that children played on others when I was in school, of the near-misses, and I think "What if?"

In your stories, women are very often ambivalent characters, both dominated by other figures and capable of atrocious acts. However, you never deny them their status as victims of a structurally sexist society. In this, you seem to follow Shirley Jackson's footsteps and it gives your stories an underlying political tone. Do you feel that the horror genre gives you the opportunity to criticize the "accepted obvious" on your own terms? Is the fictionalized violence portrayed in your stories a mirror of the real violence women are confronted with?

There is a lot of realism in my works, people aren't good or bad, and their behaviors don't usually result from a purely evil or saintly basis. For every story where we are somebody's protagonist, there is another where we are the villain. A lot of my stories are based on my experiences. I trained as a mental health nurse, and worked in forensics, and a lot of that work is focused on whether someone is mentally stable, looking at getting them to recognize and minimize their risk of relapse. You get to find out a lot about why and how people react to pressure, whether it is from their illness, societal expectations, secondary issues such as health, housing, family, or from artificial stimuli such as drugs and alcohol. A behavior that may seem unpredictable or unforgivable when you are given the facts may become more understandable once you know the person's full reasoning, no matter how unreliable s/he might be. One of the reasons I love Shirley Jackson's work is that her unreliable narrators are interesting to read because they don't know what they do or why. Then, how can the reader?

Your latest novella, *Wayside*, deals with domestic violence, both psychological and physical. In your eyes, what makes the classic gothic trope of the "couple in the mansion/manor/large house" still relevant today? What was your intention in using/reactivating it?
Although the mansion part is probably no longer that relevant, and although the house in *Wayside* is large by today's standards (a detached, country three-bed), it would have been nothing more than a farmer's cottage in the heyday of gothic fiction. The story of the woman isolated by her abusive husband is as relevant now as it was then. I've always wanted to write a gothic haunted-house story, but what swayed me on this particular tale was a comment I heard on a panel at the UK Ghost Story Festival. One of the panelists discussed options of what ghosts were and put forward the concept that a ghost was nothing more than an echo of ourselves. I really liked the idea of it being an echo, of the fact that stories are repeated, that abuse is repeated. That these are things we witness and do over and over again. I also particularly liked the idea of repercussions, of a haunting that could be both terrifying and comforting depending on whom it was obtaining its energy from. An abusive relationship gave me both that dynamic and the isolation that is so familiar within the haunted-house trope.

In your short stories and novellas, there are relatively few supernatural "monsters," although there are quite a number of supernatural events occurring in them. Are humans the most terrifying monsters? And, in your eyes, who are the worst: men or women?
I think that humans are the most terrifying monsters by far. But I think that is partly because we are more likely to come across that monster than an alien or a werewolf. If we can put ourselves into the victim's shoes, we can be terrified rather than just scared. If the monster can only kill me when I'm in space, then what do I have to fear when turning off the light in my bedroom? If you can put yourself into the perpetrator's shoes that can be even worse, what would lead you to kill? What if you killed those you loved? What if you had no choice? What if you had no control? What if you woke from your nightmare to discover that you yourself were the monster?

CHAPTER ELEVEN

Margaret Killjoy

Margaret Killjoy is an American steampunk and folk-horror writer. She is also a musician, playing across many genres. Notable works: *A Country of Ghosts* (novel, 2014), *We Won't Be Here Tomorrow* (collection, 2022).

Dear Margaret, thank you very much for accepting this interview. As you know, this book is going to focus specifically on the notions of "gender" and "genre," two very fluid notions much discussed today. In this light, can you tell us about your background and how this, in your eyes, influenced the person and the writer you are today?

Sure! I'm a white, American trans woman in her late thirties. I spent most of my adult life, until about five years ago, living a sort of transient lifestyle—hitchhiking, train-hopping, squatting, living in a van, etc.—so that I could focus on adventure and Leftist activism rather than career-building and the like. In some ways, that is as important to understanding who I am as anything about my experiences with gender and genre. But yeah, I'm a trans woman. I have been wearing women's clothes, and going by Margaret, for about twenty years now, but I only really came out as a woman maybe five years back at this point. I used to spend my time trying to broaden the category of what men can do, and while I still think that's important work, I really was just lying to myself and everyone around me, too afraid to come out as a woman.

We see today more and more nonbinary and trans writers getting mainstream recognition in speculative fiction and horror, such as for example, you, Billy Martin, April Daniels, Neon Yang, and a few others. Did you encounter any discrimination specifically related to your gender in your writing career?

I'm going to say I mostly don't, but with some caveats. I came into the more mainstream genre fiction world through a sort of side entrance: I was part of a DIY culture of zine makers and self-publishing punk weirdos, so I started off with absolutely no idea or concern about what would and wouldn't work for a broader audience. I remember though, at a convention (DragonCon in Atlanta, I don't remember what year) I asked some editors from Tor and other large presses whether or not me writing nonbinary characters and introducing they/them pronouns was likely to make my work unappealing to editors. They said, basically, absolutely not. They said they were actively looking to uplift marginalized voices and were excited about including broader gender diversity in the field. And they were telling the truth. . .Only a few years later I started selling stories and then books to more mainstream publishers and have gotten almost no pushback about it.

There are two caveats here though: first, this is only a portion of the genre fiction world. I remember, at a worldcon, a month or two before I came out, I was harassed on the street while walking back to the hotel from lunch. Not by convention-goers, just by some random man amongst his friends, who called me a word I won't reprint. Being me, I shouted him down, then walked back to the hotel. I think earlier that day I'd read about how the life expectancy for trans women in the Western hemisphere was like thirty-three or thirty-four years old . . . which is how old I was at the time. Now, those numbers don't reflect the experience of a white woman in the United States, which is one of the safest classes of trans women to be in the world, but that's still not saying much . . . I get harassed on a fairly regular basis and there are plenty of stories about how that harassment can turn to violence. So that's the mood I was in when I went into a panel and started watching some old white man pull out a string of pearls and clutch it to his neck and claim that everyone had gotten too sensitive. Too sensitive. Less than an hour after I'd had to confront a man on the street because of how he viewed how I was dressed.

So, there's that kind of thing, the last gasp of a dying generation who can't understand that "not being the only one allowed to have a voice" is not the same thing as being silenced. I think mostly people only say that kind of thing behind my back though, because, frankly, they're cowards.

The other discrimination is more subtle. There's the fact that you are held to a higher bar than other writers, especially when you write about sensitive issues. You can write "good enough" when you're not marginalized, but you've got to write damn well when you are, especially if you want to write about that marginalization directly.

Do you think trans and queer writers in horror and science fiction are in a better position today than when you began to write? Do you feel any gendered resistance in the milieu or in the reviews?
Yes and no. I mean, in some ways, who am I to tell? I only have my own experience. But I can conjecture, based on how the way I'm seen has changed over time. In general, I think it's easier to be trans in our society than it was, certainly twenty years ago, when I was too afraid to come out even to myself, when I was terrified that I might turn out to be one of those horrid, ugly trans women (I would have used a less kind word at the time). I came out in large part because of the hard work of those women I disparaged, who I was afraid to be. Seeing their courage helped me find my own, and they'd broken down an awful lot of barriers for my generation of trans folks. I'd like to think that we have broken down even more, and in the past few years there's been an explosion of people coming out of the closet and being who they always wanted to be—or even just feeling free to explore ideas of who they *might* want to be. So . . . that part is easier.

But two things are conspiring against people now. First, there's that highlander syndrome—there can only be one. I'm eternally grateful that Charlie Jane Anders, the most visible trans woman in the field when I first really entered, immediately met me positively. She knew who I was when we first met and she was kind to me. We don't keep up or anything, but seriously, eternally grateful. Socialized competition between women is a fierce and bad thing, and it's easy to find ourselves falling into it. But I also worry about . . . if our stories are included to fill quotas, then that means in some ways there *can* only be one. The answer to this isn't to broaden the quotas. It's not to go from "well this anthology should have at least two trans authors" instead of "at least one trans author." I mean, that might sometimes be part of it. But while looking to balance the scales is important, at the end of the day I think readers judge stories based on the content and quality of those stories more than the identity of the author.

I've been fairly lucky that most reviewers and readers have not lingered specifically on my own identity but instead on the content of my stories. Which often is about gender and that's good, too! Hearing from readers that they'd never seen their own gender represented in fiction before, that's an incredible feeling. The gender of characters or authors isn't completely beside the point. But I don't want to be seen as "that trans author" or "that woman author" or even "that author who writes about squatters and anarchists." Though I'd take that last one over the former two.

There is today an ongoing debate around the word "genre" in the science fiction/horror milieu. Some agree with Ursula K. Le Guin that it is socially prejudiced; others claim that it is an essential and necessary literary "identity." What is your position on the subject?
My understanding was that Le Guin refused to stop calling her work genre fiction, basically saying "it doesn't have to be a bad word," in contrast to, say, genre authors who insist on being literary.

As to where I want to be, in that debate, well, that's honestly the easiest question in the world. The labor organizer Eugene Debs has a quote that I think fits here: "While there is a lower class, I am in it, while there is a criminal element, I am of it, and while there is a soul in prison, I am not free."

If there's a gutter to write in, hell yeah, I'll write in the gutter.

If I ever write a story without any demons or magic or laser guns or anything, if I write a story about, I don't know, a librarian who can't find the book she needs to reshelve while thinking about how she misses her ex-wife and nothing happens in it; if I write the least-genre fiction imaginable, I'd still rather it somehow gets called genre fiction. Maybe, I'll throw a magical sigil on the back cover of the missing library book just so I can get seen by the readers I care more about.

Besides, the labor conditions in genre fiction are infinitely better. Whenever I talk to people who try to publish in literary (or God forbid, academic) markets, I can't help but cringe. Submission fees? Writing contests? Terrible. Writing is work. We produce content, and the world runs on content right now. If someone, anyone, is getting money off of my work, I insist that I do, too. Genre fiction understands this. God bless it.

Incidentally, I met Le Guin before I came out, and we did a presentation together in which I was wearing a skirt, long hair, and a beard, and was named Margaret, and she didn't bat an eye. Didn't bring it up, wasn't weird about it, was just engaged with what we were discussing and was encouraging of my early career. I just feel the need to shout out what an amazing and accepting person she was, every chance I get.

What is determinant in your choice of the genres you chose to write in?
Most of the time, nothing. Whatever I feel like writing. This isn't the best career move I could make . . . For a while, more of my stories were near-future science fiction about hackers and squatters, writing in a sort of half-cyberpunk vein. I saw people refer to that as basically my signature style. Before that, I wrote a fair amount of steampunk. More recently, I wrote something that is somewhere between urban fantasy and horror. I'm not trying to be like "Wow, I write in such varied modes, I'm so cool and unique." Just that . . . to me, it's all genre fiction. It's all one thing. I'm not sure where romance fits into this . . . I ghost wrote a couple of romance novels earlier on in my career when I needed the money, and have a lot of respect for the genre but haven't done it with my own stories yet.

I think the distinction between genres, like the distinction between genders, is something that only has meaning because society foists meaning onto it. I'd like to see those distinctions break down, yet at the same time I appreciate that we might cling to various social categories while trying to fight against categorization itself. Like, it's not that I think that stories with demons are better stories than stories without them. Genre isn't "better" than literature. Yet, while genre is maligned, I'm quite happy to defend it. By the same token . . . I don't actually love the concept of gender. When I'm alone, my pronouns are "I/me/my" not "she/her/hers." Gender, as I see it, is what happens when we interface with other people. And I don't like being judged by it. But, by the social categorizations that we have in place, I think "woman" is more suited to me. There's some complexity here I'm not perfectly equipped to handle, about what that means in terms of sex (in contrast to gender), about how I grew up wishing I was a girl. I just wanted to be pretty and hang out with other girls, and the closest I got was sitting out gym class in the corner with some goth girls painting our nails. I'm grateful for that little glimpse of a girlhood that teenage weirdo girls let me have with them.

I know that's tangential, but somehow it feels related to me. There are these social categories, and they're absolute garbage, but they're also sometimes useful.

Do you feel that speculative fiction and horror offer better opportunities to challenge social conventions, especially gender, and to explore alternative sexualities and alliances?
Well, you can go larger in your metaphors when you work in genre fiction. In a literary story, I might tell the story of a girl realizing she's a girl and what that might mean for her, which is great and has purpose! But what if I want her to run across a whole underground network of badass women of all types who are trying to topple patriarchy and drop out of social conventions? Suddenly, I'm probably writing genre, because that rarely happens in real life (at least how I'm imagining this story in my head, where there are rifles involved). So now I'm writing social science fiction, where the change isn't technological but one of social categorization. But what if that dramatically influences power? Frankly, I think stories that are honest about how power works are often horror. Like, my first horror novella, I didn't set out to write horror. I just set out to write a fantasy story set in modern Iowa where there's magic. And that, basically, is gonna make for horror. Because power does awful things.

I don't really think speculative fiction or horror are better than literature in terms of how they can talk about this stuff, but I'll say that they can do so differently. It's going to take all of us. Or to just admit I'm trying to quote Diane di Prima here: "NO ONE WAY WORKS / it will take all of us / shoving at the thing from all sides / to bring it down."

The several subcategories that emerged with regard to speculative fiction (gay, lesbian, transgender, feminist, black, etc.), enhanced by the different anthologies that we can find in the market, not only signify the portrayal of specific identities or communities, but also each of them seems to address a specific audience. Do you write with a gendered/nongendered audience in mind?

I honestly don't. I don't mind that people do! But I write usually for either myself or for a sort of ideal reader. If I'm writing for myself, it's because I don't know what I'm trying to say yet, and I'm just trying to figure it out. Other times, I pick a person—often a partner, if I'm being honest—and write with that person in mind. What would they like to read? How do I say what I want to say in a way that carries meaning to that person?

I find that that expands outward easily enough. If you write for a single person to understand, instead of just writing for yourself (you already know what you're trying to say, most of the time), then you can write clearly enough that some people will be able to get something out of it. It's like . . . okay, I'm in this black metal band that doesn't have any men in it, called Feminazgul. We set out to write feminist black metal, and then it turns out that a huge number of our fans are cis men. That's great! We're not writing for them, but we're not writing *not* for them (well, some of our album names might put off some cis men but so it goes). So, we just try to write what we consider to be true and earnest and powerful and meaningful, and I think people can connect to that.

You grow up and all the stories are about white boys. If you're not a white boy, you're expected to learn how to see yourself in that white boy enough that you can still enjoy the story. It never works the other way around, but it should. White boys are taught that they can see themselves in, I don't know, robots from Mars who ride dinosaurs, but not Black girls in the suburbs or something. If I write about a trans woman, I'm not writing for trans women. I'm writing for readers, who should learn the skill of seeing themselves in other people's shoes. That's the whole point of reading, anyhow. And I think most people are smart enough to get that.

Do you think that speculative fiction and horror works are differently structured when addressed to traditionally under-portrayed individuals or communities?
I'm honestly not sure. I do know that the better authors, who come from various marginalized or under-portrayed communities, do more than just say "This character has brown skin" or whatever. Different cultures—ethnic or chosen, like a queer scene—are fundamentally different spaces in some ways, and of course that will carry over into the book. I remember hearing from a Latinx author how much he hates how characters in white books never

talk to their families. That's not just a single plot point of difference, though, right? Like "a demon is stalking me in this garden, I better call my mom and get her take on all of this" might fundamentally change the book. Or, if I write about a trans woman, there's this whole thing happening underneath—when she meets people, they have all of these assumptions about her based on how well she passes, how long they've known her, what they think of trans people, etc., and that's more than characterization, that fundamentally changes what one chooses to do and what happens to someone. So, in that case, it's less about who it's addressed to, and more about the perspective of the author—or their understanding of the perspective of their characters.

Is the portrayal of a minority specifically addressed to those that feel portrayed in these works?
Huh. Once again, I think I don't do this consciously, because I'm not writing a trans woman protagonist for the sake of writing for a trans woman reader. I'm writing one because I want more representation, or because I want to write in easy mode where the protagonist has similar concerns as I do personally, or just because I like the idea of a specific character and she happens to be a trans woman. But that said, I'm writing with the trans woman reader in mind when I write a character like that. I want people to feel like characters are real, so if I write a soldier, I hope that a soldier who reads it either feels seen or feels like her friends are seen or something. There's this whole cliché about how men write women characters, and it's true, and authors should avoid replicating those problems.

In your novel, your main characters are either gay, as in *A Country of Ghosts*, or trans women, as in *The Lamb Will Slaughter the Lion* and *The Barrow Will Send What it May*, which constitute the Danielle Cain series. Do you feel that genre is more open to fluid character identities than "established literature"?
I haven't really tried to write literature, so I'm not too sure. If I did write literature, it would be full of gay and trans folks, because those are the people I'm around the most and know best. And then, it would just be a matter of whether or not people buy it. But I expect that yes, I have some more leeway in genre fiction, because to use my example above, if the reader goes into it prepared to see himself in the robot from Mars who rides dinosaurs, he probably

won't have too much of a problem with the main character liking to fuck other dudes. I'd hope so, anyway.

In your novels, anarchism is a central topic. All your characters and stories are set within anarchist communities, whether in the real world, such as your Danielle Cain series, or in a lo-fi steampunk setting, such as in *A Country of Ghosts*. How important are anarchist politics in your choice of genre and sexual identities in your fiction?
Well, I'm just lucky, honestly, in that since I come from an anarchist background, and anarchism is so welcoming to gender deviants and queers, that I never really worried about it. If I want a character to be somewhere where no one will bat an eye at their gender presentations, an anarchist commune isn't a bad place for it. Which isn't to say anarchism is inherently utopian or perfect—both those books are exactly about what is and isn't utopian about anarchism. Just that those of us rejected by mainstream society often find a home in an anarchist community. That said, I'm certain I could do the same thing in tons of other communities, and also all writing is a bit of magic, a bit of invoking. By writing about a specific community accepting trans people, I'm part of casting a spell for that community to accept trans people.

One could consider your Danielle Cain series as a queer anarchist "Buffy the Vampire Slayer" and *A Country of Ghosts* as a subtle tribute to Ursula Le Guin's *The Dispossessed*. Is that a way, for you, beyond the possible homage, to subvert classical tropes and themes?
I love tropes, and I love how genre fiction really revels in tropes. It's kind of like drag, or gender-as-performance, actually. You can signify a lot of things with subtle cues. If you find a trope you like, you can consume media that revels in that trope for days or weeks or years without getting bored. There's always something new to say about vampires or werewolves or whatnot. I mean, editors might not agree, and you might have trouble selling stories about really worn-in tropes, but there's always room for original takes. I think all you really need to do is . . . apply a unique experience or unique point of view to existing tropes. I couldn't have rewritten *The Dispossessed* if I'd tried, because my experience of anarchism is so different from Le Guin's. Not contrary to hers, by any means, just different. So, if I write an anarchist utopia, it's going to be

different. With Danielle Cain, I actually see it more as punk rock Scooby-Doo than Buffy, but that's because I actually never watched Buffy. But that's still the same trope in some ways: modern-day demon hunters.

I rarely set out to write something as a response to something else, or a riff on it, but the media you consume lives in your head rent-free and informs the sorts of stories you come up with, and I'm glad that genre fiction doesn't try to pretend like that's not the case. It's like "formulaic plot structure" which everyone critiques speculative fiction for. Who fucking cares? I built a cabin once in the woods and lived in it for a few years. I didn't invent how to build the house. I used an existing structural style, an A-frame, because it was strong and simple. And I stick-framed it, using books about how to build a house to do so. It's literally a formula. "If your walls are this tall, this is how thick the wood needs to be" or whatever. That house was unique. Even if it hadn't been, my experience living in it was unique. There are a lot of ways to build a house, and they're useful for different environments, different budgets, different purposes. But there are still only so many ways to build a house. Yet, every house (almost every house) is unique. There are a lot of plot structures, or formulas if you insist, and they're damn good ways to build stories. Unique stories.

CHAPTER TWELVE

Kathe Koja

Kathe Koja (born in 1960) is an American horror and speculative fiction writer. She also writes YA historical fiction and literary fiction. Notable works: *The Cipher* (novella, 1991), *Dark Factory* (novel, 2022).

Dear Kathe Koja, thank you very much for accepting to be part of this volume, which will focus specifically on the notions of "gender" and "genre." In this light, can you tell us about your background and how this, in your eyes, influenced the person and the writer you are today?
I'm a Detroit native, from a blue-collar background, so class is nearly as potent a determinant for me as gender. I don't see writing as a rarefied, MFA-conferred profession, I see it as making, and making is work. As a writer, I'm almost entirely self-taught, primarily by reading everything I could access from a very young age, and writing ditto; the first writing teachers I encountered were at the Clarion Workshop in the mid-1980s, when I was twenty-four, attending as a recipient of the Susan C. Petrey scholarship. That workshop focused on speculative fiction/fantasy, which drew me, as those were genres I was interested in and actively reading, though not exclusively.

My own work has crossed and recrossed many genre borders: I've written speculative fiction and horror, historical fiction, YA fiction, and now immersive fiction, an emerging genre in its own right. I've also adapted and created work for live performance, another branching genre.

Do you think women in horror and speculative fiction are in a better position today than when you began to write? Do you feel any gendered resistance in the milieu or in the reviews?
Better position creatively, or commercially? I know I've read (and been interviewed for) many, many "Women in Horror" articles in the last thirty years, and some of the same pointless hurdles persist.

What I look toward, and am thrilled and encouraged to see, are writers and editors and anthologists and reviewers who are women, who by their presence and their works' presence continue to enlarge and enrich the genres in which they work—and not only in speculative/weird/horror but every genre. Until we are the baseline, there will be work to do.

Did you encounter any discrimination specifically related to your gender in your writing career?
Every time a male voice tries to talk over mine, on a panel, in the world, there it was. And it was. And it is.

There is today an ongoing debate around the word "genre" in the science fiction/horror milieu. Some agree with Ursula K. Le Guin that it is socially prejudiced; others claim that it is an essential and necessary literary "identity." What is your position on the subject?
As a writer, I've never identified through or with any particular genre, though I've enjoyed working/playing in many. To me they're all ongoing parties, and I like to go to parties and meet new people with new points of view, that teach me new ways to see and understand, and recreate the world on the page. And I've always been welcomed in those genres by readers generous enough to take a risk on a new byline.

As a professional, I've seen genre perceived/used as an economic sieve, a stick to beat people with, a safety net, a badge of honor, a slur, the list goes on.

Your fiction is often a hybrid of different genres: horror, speculative fiction, weird, and others. What is determinant in your choice of these genres, and in mixing them?
I don't make a conscious choice of genre when I write, or plan what I'm going to write, and I love the surprise of that, the creative stretch, the confusion, and the glee: it's how I wrote *Under the Poppy*/historical fiction, *Skin*/horror fiction, *Talk*/YA fiction, *Dark*

Factory/immersive fiction. The only exceptions would be short stories written as a response to an editor's invitation to submit to an anthology, where you know the brief going in.

How did you choose to write horror? Was it a conscious decision?
My first novel, *The Cipher*, originally began as an outgrowth of a short speculative fiction story called "Distances." That story got some good attention, was included on best-of lists and anthologies, and my then-agent suggested I enlarge it into a novel. I tried to do that, totally failed, but was drawn to one of the characters and decided to excise him from the stagnant manuscript and see what happened. That character was Nicholas, around whom the Funhole accreted, grew, and brought the darkness with it. My agent offered that book to Jeanne Cavelos for the seminal Dell Abyss line, and it became a horror novel.

One of your most famous novels, *The Cipher*, deals directly with the notion of "body horror." Would you see it, from your perspective, as a gendered genre, even though the main character, Nicholas, is male?
Body horror pertains and belongs to anyone who has a body. The ways the horror manifests can be, and often are, gendered—sometimes catastrophically so, history as well as fiction shows us that over and over—but at baseline we're all just meat afraid of the knife, afraid of the pain, afraid of the dissolution that all meat eventually has to endure.

What writers have you been influenced by? Was their gender important to you?
Emily Brontë and Shirley Jackson were hugely influential for me—I read *Wuthering Heights* at ten years old, and have never stopped reading it—and across the board, the writers who drew me were always at home in places and states of intensity, like Plath, and Poe. Neither gender nor genre were really guides to what I read—as a young reader, I was probably much more aware of the characters' gender than the writers'!—and reading great writers led me to read more great writers.

The several subcategories that emerged with regard to horror (gay, lesbian, transgender, feminist, black, etc.), enhanced by the different anthologies that we can find in the market, not only signify the portrayal of specific identities or communities, but also each of them seems to address a specific audience. Do you write with a gendered audience in mind?

Experience as a reader and as a writer has taught me that the story finds its reader, always: it may take a while, but if a story out there is yours, speaks to you, belongs to you, it will find you. It's best if you're already out there looking, too, of course! But the voices that are yours will always be yours: it's why we feel that happy shock, that joy of recognition, when we read a piece of fiction that seems to speak directly to us, that seems as if it was written just for us: because in the deepest sense, it was.

In many of your stories, including your latest novel, *Dark Factory*, art, in its many forms, seems to play a great role in establishing nonconformist identity or identities. Would you consider genre as art, in that it goes against mainstream representations and tropes?

What's sold as art and practiced as art may be two different things, or twenty different things. Or the same thing. And we know that popularity is not a bellwether of quality, a thing made can be wonderful *and* wonderfully popular, or it can be simplistic crap and just as popular. But because capitalism wants to define what art is and dispense the funds to make it, at times, a lot of the time, art has to live by its own rules just to survive.

Although the question of gender doesn't seem to occupy a central role in your fiction, are you aware of its implications when you write a story? Do you choose the main or secondary characters according to gender, or do you feel it's "random"?

For me, the characters are organic to the story, novel, performance, whatever I might be making, so they've already chosen themselves, and it's my job to see and understand them, then depict them as faithfully and accurately as I can, and of course gender will be a large part of who they are.

I have been asked why I write about queer characters so often, a question no one has ever asked me about characters who are not.

In *Velocities*, your latest short-story collection, you present a large range of genres, from psychological to classical, body and even speculative fiction-inspired horror, to name a few. Do you feel that this reflects your personality as a writer?

I think it reflects the variety of characters that carried with them the stories in *Velocities*—and more than a few of those were written as a response to an editor's invitation. One of my favorite voices in that collection, one of my favorite characters ever, the amoral and terrifying Pearlie of "La Reine d'Enfer," exists because **Ellen Datlow** and Terri Windling invited me to write a story for *Queen Victoria's Book of Spell*s, an anthology of gaslamp fantasy, a subgenre that was totally new to me.

Dark Factory **seems in many ways inspired by Andy Warhol's "Factory" project, which ran from 1963 to 1987, and whose aim was "total art." You both pursued and reinvented the project by giving the reader the possibility of being part of the story through access to various media, websites, online events, etc. This possibility both gives your book its specific identity, but also creates the need for a new genre or literary category, such as a** *roman total,* **in which reality would be an active part of the fiction. Did you have the intention of breaking "genre" itself when you began on this novel? Did you expect this result?**
I truly didn't know what to expect! *Dark Factory* has been the most baffling, fulfilling, and demanding project I have ever worked on—in its shape is its reason, but it took me a *long* time to understand what that shape was, and how a story could play with, and across, platforms, and offer ways to be involved in that play, to readers and to other artists. The artists I've been fortunate enough to attract—visual artists, musicians, filmmakers, a scent creator, a muralist, a VR maven, and more to come—have done work that amazes aesthetically while it also furthers the world of the story, absolutely a *roman total,* immersive fiction. And what's most exciting about immersive fiction as a genre is the ways that readers can use it. We're used to interacting with our media now, so this is a genre that belongs fully to its time.

And this project found its perfect home with **Tricia Reeks**, at Meerkat Press. Tricia was and is fearless, she dove immediately into the concept, and we worked together to define how *Dark Factory*—and now its companion fiction, *Dark Park*—could exist. Finding ways to enlarge and reimagine genres is not what we might automatically assume is the proper work of publishing, but of course it is, and Tricia proves that conclusively.

CHAPTER THIRTEEN

Anya Martin

Anya Martin is an American horror writer and co-host and producer of The Outer Dark podcast. Notable works: *Sleeping With Monsters* (collection, 2018).

Dear Anya Martin, thank you very much for accepting to answer these few questions. This book is going to focus specifically on the notions of "gender" and "genre" as we believe that both are equally intersectional and are either confronted by or confronting territorial positions of dominance. In this light, can you tell us about your background and how this, in your eyes, influenced the person and the writer you are today?

Thank you for asking me to participate in this vitally important discussion. That's a big question, but I'll try to answer it succinctly here, knowing that later questions will expand upon this answer. First, I was fortunate to be born to two intellectual and creative parents who taught me not only to have empathy for all humanity and animals, but also to approach dogmatic statements with skepticism and analytic thinking. In other words, my household was both intrinsically "speculative" and "imaginative."

I grew up in the suburban United States, mostly (from second grade/age seven) in Atlanta at a time when it was rapidly evolving from a Southern capital into an international regional metropolis. My dad was a bookish kid from small-town Kentucky and Tennessee who expanded his horizons by serving in the Second World War. Under the GI Bill, he became the only one of eight siblings to go to university and went all the way to earn a PhD in sociology. As a much-loved and respected professor, he believed fervently in civil/ human rights, unions, and community organization. After I was born, he rediscovered his childhood love of science fiction and horror and passed that on to me. Later, he would encourage me to start a science fiction club at my high school (literally both the end and start of my social life!), and he became a member of science fiction's First Fandom organization. Thanks to him, I grew up in a house with books in every room, and most of the gifts under our Christmas tree were books.

My mother was Finnish with two master's degrees, in political science and library science, and ultimately rose to a management position at the Coca-Cola Company's technical library. As a leader in Atlanta's Finnish and Scandinavian organizations, she was always organizing multicultural exhibits, conferences, and social events. My mother was skeptical of science fiction as serious literature, but she also encouraged reading—folk- and fairy tales, *Anne of Green Gables*, and most of all the Moomins series by Tove Jansson. She wrote stories, letters, and family histories, and translated Finnish and Swedish fiction into English.

My childhood was full of reading (books and comics), pretend games, which often included witches and superheroines, and international community activities. I was always writing stories, plays (some of which were produced at school or in backyards), and the beginnings of novels. In a kind of wish-fulfillment, I guess, all centered on prominent women characters, including screenplays to *Star Wars* sequels.

Both of my parents encouraged me to believe that women could do anything to which their hopes and dreams aspired. There was never any question in our home whether I would go to college or that higher education was not something women did. I earned a bachelor's degree in anthropology at Smith College and a master's in communication (print journalism) at Georgia State University, because that seemed a good idea for someone who wanted to be a writer. Of course, like many, I found that journalism taps from the same well as fiction, so for many years, the overwhelming majority of my time was devoted to writing nonfiction, along with some public relations work in comics, film, and healthcare. That being said, I credit journalism with advancing my craft, teaching me to write quickly and to pick my words with laser precision.

You are a journalist, a horror writer, and the co-organizer of The Outer Dark podcast, as well as the event called The Outer Dark Symposium on The Greater Weird. As a woman, did you encounter any difficulties specifically related to your gender in your career as a horror writer, podcast producer, and event organizer?

Alas, sadly, of course, the answer is yes, and also in my journalism career. Some are obvious examples of sexism or other inappropriate advances, but I'd like to talk about one example that is subtle, but extremely significant because it is impossible to prove conclusively. Yet, many women I have spoken with share similar experiences, and it's come up regularly in panel discussions at conventions including at The Outer Dark Symposium, and on the podcast.

When I first started submitting stories to horror and spec-lit magazines and anthologies in the 1990s, editors (mostly men, but some women, too) complimented my "good writing" but passed because the story "didn't fit." These submissions weren't directed to theme anthologies but to magazines or anthologies that advertised themselves as being "cutting edge" or expanding the boundaries of horror. A case in point was "A Girl and Her Dog," a story that started with watching my dog "run" in his sleep and led to me thinking about what one might give up to increase a dog's lifespan. I don't want to give spoilers about any story endings but only to say that the tone/action is subtly disturbing rather than overtly horrific.

Sometimes I got suggestions that, if followed, would in my view make the story more conventional and strip it of what I felt made it work. One editor said he didn't "understand" the story, which completely floored and confused me. Someone else felt it should be about a cat instead, as if girls never bonded with dogs. Another felt the title demanded it be a direct response to Harlan Ellison's "A Boy and His Dog." Yes, I had intentionally named the story in tandem with Ellison's story after I completed it, but my point was that it literally is a "different" story. Still, as one reader recently said to me, in both stories, a choice is made to sacrifice something to save the dog. In Ellison's story, the boy literally kills a girl, but in my story, I hate to give spoilers about how or what, but my girl protagonist sacrifices a piece of herself.

Beta readers, many of whom were accomplished published authors, told me "A Girl and Her Dog" was a strong and compelling story, but at some point, I stopped submitting it. Years later in 2013, at NecronomiCon Providence, Rhode Island, I discovered a then-blossoming community of contemporary Weird fiction writers and editors. Suddenly, more subtle and strange horror was being published, and a new generation of small press editors were actively looking for women writers to submit. I dug it out again, made some very minor copyedits, and the next year, Jordan Krall, of Dunhams Manor Press, accepted "A Girl and Her Dog" for publication in the second issue of *Xynobis*, a Weird fiction journal.

What changed? One clue might be found in a number of instances over the past few years when editors have been called out on social media for the paucity of women writers in an anthology's table of contents. Some editors acknowledged that perhaps they didn't try hard enough with outreach to women writers. But others dug their heels in and insisted that stories written by women simply weren't as good as the stories submitted by male authors. Sometimes, they added, like a badge of honor, that they read "blind" submissions. Or, they pointed to the women writers they had already published and for whose careers they even seemed to take credit. One such editor recently said something like that to my face when I neglected to mention his anthology on a panel.

Reading between the lines, it's hard not to wonder, as many women spec-lit authors I know do, what it would have been like had not these gatekeepers been so rigidly set in their definition of what a good "whatever genre" story is. Could it be that some women's stories were published because they fitted within these boundaries or only marginally stretched them? Conversely, the great stories that were never published, the authors we never would know. "A Girl and Her Dog" was rejected because it "didn't fit." Multiply this effect when a woman of color is the author. No matter what editors and publishers say publicly about wanting to push boundaries, these gatekeepers need to be open to a different story—a different kind of story. But honestly why would anyone want to keep reading the same story all her life? Isn't the point of "speculative fiction" not to be solely comfort food?

What do you think of the position of women in horror and science fiction today compared to the 1950s, when Ursula Le Guin and C. J. Cherryh had to hide the fact they were women in order to get published? Do you feel any gender-based resistance in the milieu or in the reviews?

Well, thanks to my dad, I actually had a skewed view of how many women were writing science fiction and horror and how much sexism was in the genre. He was always directing me toward women authors like C. L. Moore, Leigh Brackett, Mary Elizabeth Counselman, Ursula K. Le Guin, Kate Wilhelm, Anne McCaffrey, C. J. Cherryh, Katherine Kurtz, Hope Mirlees, Andre Norton, Jane Yolen, and Joanna Russ. Vonda N. McIntyre's *Dreamsnake* and Joan D. Vinge's *Snow Queen* were so important to me. In editing, Betty Ballantine, Judy-Lynn del Rey, and **Ellen Datlow** were household names.

On a side note, it's really exciting to see the work of researchers like Lisa Yaszek, Regents Professor of Science Fiction Studies at Georgia Tech in Atlanta. Yaszek has been debunking the narrative that the majority of women used initials or pseudonyms in science fiction, though certainly some did. Also, when one reviews publication lists from the pulps, while men predominate, women definitely were writing science fiction and horror from the 1930s through the 50s. For example, although certain gatekeepers have made sure that Lovecraft Circle authors are thus far much better remembered, at least some classic *Weird Tales* magazine authors were definitely women. It's been exciting to see all the recent efforts to recover women authors, such as Valancourt's *The Women of Weird Tales* and Scott Nicolay's "Stories from the Borderlands" blog posts, on which I assisted with editing and some research. Lisa Yaszek's two-volume *The Future is Female!* anthologies for Library of America are a must read! And *Astounding* by Alec Nevala-Lee illuminated the pivotal behind-the-scenes roles of Doña Stewart and Leslyn MacDonald, the wives of editor John W. Campbell and writer Robert A. Heinlein in their Golden Age success. Recovering lost women writers (and editors) is a really important work, and I hope to be able to devote more time to it.

That being said, publishing opportunities and roads to recognition for women certainly are much better today in 2022, even if we still have ground to cover (for example, what I said about some remaining entrenched gatekeeper editors in the previous answer). In the 2022 Hugo Awards, all the prose fiction writing categories went to women. Also, in recent years, it's been gratifying to see so many women and nonbinary people of color win spec-lit awards such as N. K. Jemisin, Nisi Shawl, **Eugen Bacon**, zin e. rocklyn, and Sheree Renée Thomas, who is now the editor of *The Magazine of Fantasy and Science Fiction*. Increasingly anthology, magazine, and year's best editors seem to be consciously trying to achieve gender balance and to be far more open to diverse and intersectional perspectives. That being said, the small press continues to take the lead and be the place to find the most cutting-edge genre fiction by women. Some notable presses publishing phenomenal women Weird fiction authors include Undertow, Word Horde, Erewhon, Meerkat, Dim Shores, Broken Eye, Small Beer, Mythic Delirium, PM, and Tachyon.

Still, urban fantasy and YA aside, major US publishing houses do not always give women horror authors the same level of marketing support as they give to established or new male authors. Still, it's been heartening to witness the huge success of Canadian-based Mexican author Silvia Moreno-Garcia and to see other notable cutting-edge women horror authors among the recent Big Five books including Cassandra Khaw, Gwendolyn Kiste, Veronica Shanoes, Ruthanna Emrys, Kristi DeMeester, zin e. rocklyn, and Damien Angelica Walters.

So, in many ways, now is arguably the most exciting time to be a woman writer of spec-lit and horror, but it's also important not to erase the women before us who contributed with amazing work and lent their perspective to the genre. In addition, big strides to break the glass ceiling are still clearly needed for women genre film directors and screenwriters, as well as comics creators.

There is today an ongoing discussion about "genre." Some say it doesn't exist, others claim that it is an essential literary identity. What is your position on the subject? Do you see genre as a symbolic prison or as a space of freedom?
I don't have a problem with "genre" as an organizational term or a marketing convenience. I still head to the science fiction and fantasy section of bookstores or online retailers. Certainly, where genre becomes problematic is when it is used in a negative sense, e.g., because a work is "sci-fi" or "horror," it cannot be "serious literature." Now that science fiction, fantasy, and horror are being reviewed in the *New York Review of Books* and genre dominates mass media, this stigma is hopefully becoming less relevant.

I principally identify as a Weird fiction writer, and for me, this is a space of freedom because I don't see The Weird as a genre but as a mode that transcends genre. In other words, The Weird can be present in horror, science fiction, fantasy, or realistic literary fiction. Weird fiction once was overly associated with Lovecraft and cosmic horror—i.e., the white male protagonist versus a tentacled monster in a universe that doesn't care about humanity. Again, thank the gatekeepers for this narrow view. But that definition and limited expectation was dynamited by such developments as **Ann VanderMeer**'s phenomenal and controversial run as editor of *Weird Tales* magazine in the 2000s, the diverse and far-reaching table of contents in *The Weird* anthology edited by **Ann VanderMeer** and Jeff VanderMeer (2012), the rise of contemporary Weird fiction small presses actively seeking "different" stories, and *Year's Best Weird Fiction* volumes from Undertow Publications.

When **Kathe Koja** edited the second volume of the latter (2015), she described The Weird as undefinable and that "I know it when I see it." That characterization may seem too vague, but it's really surprisingly clear when you realize that the story changes when the author changes. Lovecraft's Weird was almost bereft of women and embedded in racist fear of The Other. But The Weird may not be so terrifying to a marginalized author and even may provide a source of strength or hope. I was on a "Women in Weird Fiction" panel at the end of The Outer Dark Symposium in 2019, where other women echoed the sense that the emergence of a contemporary Weird Renaissance (to use the term coined by Scott Nicolay, with whom I co-host/co-produce The Outer Dark podcast) had created a space for us, independent of genre marketing in the publishing industry. In The Weird, suddenly all things are possible, regardless of gender, color, sexual orientation, or any other marginalizing characteristic and what could be more exciting!

Did you choose the genre of horror, or did it choose you?
I guess it chose me in that I don't remember a time when I didn't gravitate toward horror and especially monsters. From age two, I watched the *Dark Shadows* soap opera, featuring vampire Barnabas Collins, and by age seven, I was obsessed with Friday Night Frights movie nights on local Channel 17, which would later grow into Turner Broadcasting and spawn CNN. Before I graduated elementary school, I had seen all the major Universal, Hammer, AIP, and Toho monster movies. I was almost never scared and usually empathized with the misunderstood monster, whether Frankenstein's creation or King Kong. I'm pretty sure I cried the first time I saw the 1933 original *King Kong*.

Halloween was my favorite holiday, trick or treating much more exciting than Christmas, and my guidebook was Ray Bradbury's

The Halloween Tree. Many of my favorite books were about witches, such as Eleanor Estes's *The Witch Family*, and I had a whole make-believe game based around a witch called Lucia who had a wand called "the white flag." I knew the location along the bus route to downtown Atlanta's most notorious local haunted mansion. One of my dad's sociology colleagues taught me to read Tarot cards. I even filmed a horror show called "Mr. Hyde's Castle" in sixth grade.

That being said, again I now identify more strongly as a Weird fiction writer than a horror writer, though certainly a deep sense of unease, destabilization, and horror runs through my work. Almost all of my stories are horror in some respect, and my collection's title should tell you I am still very interested in what monsters can teach us.

You have written and published many short stories over the years and your first collection, *Sleeping with the Monster*, came out in 2018. The red thread in this very diverse collection of stories is that all main protagonists are women. Is this how you constructed your book?
I didn't consciously plan my first collection only to include stories from a female point of view, but I am completely comfortable that it came out that way. I should point out that technically "Old Tsah-Hov" is narrated by a male street dog in Jerusalem, though his fate is tied to the woman who adopts him and takes him with her to the United States. That story was originally written for *Cassilda's Song*, an all-woman anthology of stories inspired by Robert W. Chambers's *The King in Yellow* cycle and edited by the late Joseph S. Pulver, Sr. I remain grateful to Joe for taking a chance on publishing a Weird tale that shares thematic similarities to those works rather than overtly using characters or places in its "mythos."

When I put together the table of contents, I did consider whether I should add a story with a male protagonist. But then, I asked myself "Why?" As a reader, I never found enough "representation" of realistic women protagonists in the spec-lit and horror that I read. So, if I did my small part in increasing more representation of realistic/believable women characters in horror, so be it.

Do you think that women have a special function in horror narratives?
I'm pretty uncomfortable with "specific function" based on gender in any kind of stories. The most effective stories, in any genre or

literature, illuminate something about the human condition. My interest is in reading and writing stories about "real" women that real women will identify with, and so anyone else can perhaps better understand and empathize with the real lived experiences of women. We should be characters, not caricatures.

Nevertheless, in horror fiction and film historically, women often have been relegated to a limited number of tropes. Familiar examples include the victim who must be rescued from the monster by the male hero, the mother fighting the monster to save her child, the "bad" girl who is punished for liking sex by being killed by the monster (or who may temporarily be made into a monster herself, such as a vampire bride), the evil mother (or the mother who inspires an evil son), the wicked witch (which can serve either as sex object or as a marker for our distrust of the wisdom of middle-aged/senior women), and of course, the "final girl"—which may or may not be a form of female empowerment. In many cases, mainstream male horror writers also have made their female protagonist a "recovering" rape victim. While such a story may sound like an equalizing good deed, it has often, alas, become a reductionist trope of its own.

Oh, and then there's the one "tomboy" in a group of young boys, who creepily serves also as a form of titillation for them. I don't think I need to name the most famous example of that one, if you are at all familiar with contemporary bestselling horror. A couple of years earlier, I posed a question on social media as to whether anyone could name a horror story/novel/film that was centered around a group of grade school girls. The absence of even one clear example was stunning. Meanwhile, there are plenty of examples of horror stories about lone little girls, or girls with one bestie or a cat. In my own "little girl" experience, I was part of a group of four female friends and slumber party seances, ghost stories, pretending we were witches, and creek exploration adventures were among the top things we did for fun. So, in direct response to the absence of girl-group-centered stories, I wrote "All the Things We Need to Kill Squissshh" (*Cooties Shot Required*, Broken Eye Books, 2020), a Weird tale about four monster-movie-loving fourth-grade friends who plot to destroy a monster together without the help of any boys. I'm working on another story about the same girls in what I hope will be a sequence.

I do think it's important to confront and give voice to women characters in horror, similar to how contemporary women authors have explored and expanded the perspectives of fairy-tale villains. Recent years have seen many great examples such as Silvia Moreno-Garcia's *The Daughter of Doctor Moreau* and Gwendolyn Kiste's *Reluctant Immortals*. I admit I have done it in several other stories, including "The Un-Bride, or No Gods and Monsters" (*Eternal Frankenstein*, Word Horde, 2016). That novella is pretty overtly feminist in that it postulates that actress Elsa Lanchester gave film director James Whale a true story on which to model *Bride of Frankenstein* (1935), a movie that for its time challenged horror tropes and was based on a book by a woman (Mary Shelley) that still stands out for the many levels on which it operates. It is worth remembering and repeating that in many ways Mary Shelley is the progenitor of both the science fiction and horror genres as we know them today.

In your latest collection, all stories belong to a different genre, from urban horror to gothic. Is this a deliberate choice or is it the way you see yourself as a writer, free from categories?
Again, I see myself as a writer using the mode of Weird fiction which is cross-genre. That's how I pitched the collection to my editor Steve Berman, at Lethe Press, and I hope readers also see this connection. That being said, I did not include some stories because they are not Weird or relevant to the title, such as "The Courage of the Lion Tamer" (*Daybreak*, online magazine), an optimistic future "what if" science fiction story set in Kenya about wild animal conservation, or "The Toe," a brutally realistic horror flash fiction about a date gone horribly wrong. I definitely did not consider the terms "urban horror" or "gothic" when writing these stories, but I can see how readers might see some of them this way.

To me, exploring the weirdness of real life is exactly what Weird horror does best. H. P. Lovecraft, his circle, and his literary descendants may consider cosmic horror on a macro scale, similar to noir crime fiction, through the viewpoint of a lone alienated white male protagonist. But a growing subgenre has emerged of what might be termed as micro "domestic" cosmic horror. This mode has been used powerfully by authors whom Lovecraft would have termed "The Other," whether women, queer, disabled, people of color, etc. When life gets Weird, fully realistic fiction can catalog and chronicle the blatant aspects, but the weirdness stays with you, embeds in your skin, creates discomfort in the deepest recesses of the brain, and changes your daily life so that routine becomes therapy and nothing ever feels the same "normal" again.

Horror author, anthologist, and critic Douglas E. Winter has said, "Horror is an emotion." In Weird horror, that emotion is often characterized as simply dread. But dread isn't simple, and The Weird as a literary mode is uniquely suited to address its complexity from a variety of diverse perspectives in which the lines between good and evil blur and the "monster" is not necessarily the central villain, if the story happens to have a villain in the traditional sense.

I titled my first collection, *Sleeping with the Monster*, but I didn't set out to write a "cycle" of stories that were cohesive. Yet, in one way or another, I realized every tale had a monster, whether the Evil Man in "A Girl and Her Dog" or the bugs in "Boisea Trivittata." The presence of monsters is pretty explicit in stories, such as "Grass" or "Black Stone Roses and Granite Gazanias," and multiple monsters are present in "The Prince of Lyghes" and "Jehessimin." In other tales, it's up to the reader to decide who or what the real monster is, whether it's a creature or a person, sympathetic or villain, or even a more neutral means to some kind of imperfect salvation.

Do you write with a gendered audience in mind? Do you create your characters with a specific message or intention regarding the readers?

As noted previously, representation is important for women readers, so on some level, like when I wrote plays and stories as a little girl, I hope that women readers will appreciate my work. That being said, I also hope male readers emerge from a story with a better idea of how women think, with more respect for women's choices, less threatened by the concept of an empowered woman, and generally more equipped to be a constructive communicator, listener, and ally.

On a broader scale, most of my stories address horrific, disturbing, or simply strange real-life experiences through the lens of the supernatural and the Weird. If I had named the collection something different, it might have included the word "illusions." I can't quote lyrics without paying song licensing, but you can search online for a song by that title sung by the marvelous Marlene Dietrich. Those lyrics might apply particularly to the play "Passage to the Dreamtime," in which an American jazz singer confronts her German general lover in prison for war crimes after the Second

World War. While it would seem obvious she was sleeping with a monster, it didn't seem like it to her at the time.

One of the scariest things about toxic relationships is the way they take on a certain day-to-day normalcy that rationalizes the horror away. People ask, well, why didn't she leave, which certainly applies to my story "The Prince of Lyghes." One reviewer called Jenny, the protagonist, "passive," but I see the way she goes with the flow of cohabiting with a dangerous husband as a self-survival strategy. No one is coming to save her from a death of one hundred pricks until something Weird happens that shatters the disturbing equilibrium, though whether it has empathy or intends to rescue is ambiguous. In "Grass," Sheila is stuck in a rut after a toxic marriage until an encounter with a Weird monster that could be worse but might also offer her exactly what she needs to move on. In "Weegee Weegee, Tell Me Do," (*Tales from a Talking Board*, Word Horde, 2017), Orlaugh's hands take matters into their own hands literally after being given an opportunity to achieve a theatrical dream.

In real life, women so often return to toxic relationships, even after separations, thinking their partner has learned something and it will somehow not be as horrible this time. Only it gets worse. But for those who do get out, freedom comes with a euphoria both energizing and strange given the rapid metamorphosis. Thus, in my stories, I wanted to use The Weird consciously to show not only stasis and struggle but also to transcend emotional and physical violence and illuminate a path out. My characters don't always get out alive and don't necessarily get out undamaged, but they do get out. I'm ever humbled by the portrayals of gender relations in Tiptree's fiction, and her "The Women Men Don't See" is a must-read example of feminist spec-lit that uses The Weird in a similar way.

In others of my own stories such as "A Girl and Her Dog" and "Jehessimin," Weird events intervene before Cassie or Angie ever gets into a deep relationship with a man. Actually "Jehessimin," which takes off from a common young woman's fantasy that she might actually be a fairy "changeling," might be my most hopeful story in the book, though in no way does it conclude with any sort of neat resolution. "Window" is a sort of ghost story about the hazards of loving someone who is still obsessed with a previous lover. In "Sensoria," Sasha finds love, loses it, and has a chance to seemingly retrieve her lover back via a hallucinogenic insect, but with pieces missing and a *giallo*-esque killer in pursuit. "Black Stone Roses and Granite Gazanias" was styled purposefully as a cautionary satire of the mainstream charming rogue or sympathetic male monster narrative and other urban fantasy/horror/gothic tropes. I'm not sure if the above examples specifically answer your question. But if I have any gender-specific hope, it's simply that my characters and tales first and foremost illuminate something about the actual lived experience of being a woman to all readers. If any story goes a step further to empower a woman, to encourage her to take charge and transform her life or to teach a man to be a more effective and understanding ally or partner, it would be tremendously satisfying.

Have some women authors especially influenced you? Would you "genderize" your influences or consider them as a unisex whole?
When I was younger, I didn't specifically differentiate between men and women authors in terms of influence. But in recent years, I have recognized how influential women authors have been on my work. Some women spec-lit authors that come immediately to mind include Angela Carter, C. L. Moore, Tanith Lee, Margaret St. Clair, Zenna Henderson, Ursula K. Le Guin, Joanna Russ, James Tiptree Jr., Octavia E. Butler, Toni Morrison, Mary Shelley, Amparo Dávila, Shirley Jackson, Chelsea Quinn Yarbro, Melanie Tem, Rosel George Brown, Jane Yolen, Leonora Carrington, and Isak Dinesen, plus the two women editors of *Weird Tales* magazine, Dorothy McIlreath and **Ann VanderMeer**. At an early age, my favorite authors included Tove Jansson (see below), Astrid Lindgren (Pippi Longstocking books), Frances Hodgson Burnett (*A Secret Garden*), Eleanor Estes (*The Witch Family*), Lucy Maud Montgomery (*Anne of Green Gables*), Madeline L'Engle (*A Wrinkle in Time*), and the incredible underrated Margot Benary-Isbert (*The Wicked Enchantment*). Right now just in the Weird side of spec-lit, some women authors whose works constantly awe and energize me include **J. S. Breukelaar**, M. Rickert, Brooke Warra, Damien Angelica Walters, Kristi DeMeester, zin e. rocklyn, S. P. Miskowski, Gwendolyn Kiste, Silvia Moreno-Garcia, Selena Chambers, Tonya Liburd, **Eugen Bacon**, Molly Tanzer, Larissa Glasser, Paula Ashe, Kay Chronister, **Gemma Files**, Mariana Enríquez, Gabriela Damián Miravete, Samanta Schweblin, Monica Ojeda, Rios de la Luz, Kelly Link,

Kaaron Warren, Sarah Read, Lesley Wheeler, **Priya Sharma**, Eden Royce, Nnedi Okorafor, Nicole Givens Kurtz, Cassandra Khaw, Sumiko Saulson, Christina Sng, **Kathe Koja**, Fiona Maeve Geist, and Nancy A. Collins. I am sure I have left out as many as I included!

Your roots are American and Finnish and you still return to Finland once in a while. Do you feel that this is an important part of your identity, both as a woman and as a writer?
Yes, but I didn't necessarily see that as clearly until the last five to ten years. My mother was extremely proud to be from the world's first nation (in 1906) to grant women unrestricted rights both to vote and to run for parliament, and that Finland has had a woman president and several women prime ministers. She raised me to view modern Finland as a progressive nation that leads the world in education, public healthcare, environmental policy, not to mention architecture and design. In the past few years, unfortunately my mother suffered cognitive decline and an Alzheimer's diagnosis. But even if I can no longer ask her questions, I have been learning more about my Finnish family heritage and her life as I go through her books, photos, and papers, including letters, memoirs, and unpublished translations of Finnish books.

There's been a lot of discussion about *suomikumma* or "Finnish Weird" in the works of Leena Krohn, Johanna Sinisalo, Pasi Ilmari Jääskeläinen, Emmi Itäranta, and others. I don't think that my fiction falls exactly into that mode as embodied by their work, but I do feel a strong affinity with these writers' tales and I do seek to write women characters with *sisu*—a common Finnish word for bravery and resilience. I was really excited when Helsinki won the bid to host the World Science Fiction Convention in 2017, and I made sure that I went. It was thrilling to see the welcoming spaces created for diversity in the programming and at the Hugo Awards, which were just coming off of the Sad Puppies controversy.

My biggest Finnish literary love is for the Moomin books by Tove Jansson, which my mother read aloud to me and which I later read on my own. I have no doubt that in some way they influence who I am as a person and as a writer. For those who don't know them, the main characters are a family of hippo-like trolls and an eccentric supporting cast of peculiar humans and totally strange creatures, such as the ghost-like Groke, who at first appears to be a villain but she may just be perpetually melancholic. The series, which Jansson supplemented with a long-running comic strip, is ostensibly for children, but these books are the kind where there are lots of layers for an adult to appreciate. The stories are effused with warmth, life lessons, and an appreciation for nature, but also Weird objects drive the narratives such as a hobgoblin's hat that transforms the wearer, a floating theater, and a comet threatening to crash into Moominvalley. One could compare their sensitivity perhaps to Hiyao Miyazaki's *Totoro* or *Spirited Away*, and the Moomins actually were licensed as a Japanese anime series, spawning all kinds of merchandise.

I'm also proud to share a family connection with acclaimed Finnish writer and poet Bo Carpelan, whom I had the pleasure of meeting once at a café for spirited conversation, thanks to my mother. She translated his novel, *Voices at the Late Hour*, about a family retreat to a summer cottage after a worldwide nuclear catastrophe, perhaps a Finnish riff on Nevil Shute's *On the Beach*.

I have not thus far set any of my stories in Finland nor made any of my characters Finnish or Finnish-American, but I feel like that will happen and even possibly soon. Also, I am working on a nonfiction book which takes off from a family "secret" I discovered through letters which my parents exchanged after she returned to Finland upon completion of her master's degree at Indiana University where they met. This discovery is not spec-lit but fascinating on many levels, and I am really excited to dig into that project. As I said earlier, real life can get Weird, and perhaps there's some Finnish weirdness in this true story!

CHAPTER FOURTEEN

Angela Mi Young Hur

Angela Mi Young Hur (born 1982) is a Sweden-based Korean-born American horror writer. Notable works: *Folklorn* (novel, 2021).

Dear Angela Mi Young Hur, many thanks for accepting to be part of this volume, which will focus specifically on the notions of "gender" and "genre." In this light, can you tell us about your background and how this, in your eyes, influenced the person and the writer you are today?

My parents are Koreans who immigrated to the US in the early 1970s with their two sons. I was the only one in my family born in the US. We lived in a multiethnic, lower-middle-class suburb of Los Angeles. At age fourteen, I left home, as a scholarship student, to attend an exclusive four-year boarding school, Phillips Academy in Andover, Massachusetts. I went on to Harvard after that, then moved around the US, living in various cities and picking up an MFA from Notre Dame along the way. As a wife and mother, I've toggled back and forth between Stockholm and the US with my family.

My itinerant life has given me access to various regional, ethnic, and class communities. Unsurprisingly, my work also reflects themes of rootlessness, exploration, flight, and a search for home. I am not a refugee like my father, who fled his ancestral hometown Kaesong (in what is now North Korea) during the Korean War. But the themes of leaving home, exile, dislocation, crossing borders, and flitting through communities are certainly a large part of my writing and identity as a writer.

As a woman of color and a child of immigrants, my perspective is the one of an outsider-observer. My education and the access that provides, along with being a light-skinned Asian woman, also give me certain privileges. My societal advantages and disadvantages are constantly in flux depending on where I am, whom I'm with, and to whom I am speaking. Code-switching, adaptability, shapeshifting— these are survival skills for those crossing all sorts of borders, including those in genre. Through reinterpreting genre tropes, shifting between and hybridizing genre modes, I want to challenge reader presumptions of what an Asian-American novel is supposed to be.

By subverting reader expectations and playing with their assumptions on genre and characters of a certain background, I invite readers to also engage in shapeshifting—of their understanding of my novel's characters as well as of their own myriad selves, including identities self-constructed and imposed upon, secret or aspirational.

Do you feel any gendered resistance or stigmatization in the milieu or in the reviews?

Folklorn is my second novel, the first to be marketed as science fiction/fantasy, etc. I don't detect a gendered resistance or stigmatization in the reviews or general reception, mainly because the reviewers have been mostly, almost exclusively, women. The book has been reviewed by a few male critics for their blogs, but as far as I know the reviewers for magazines or newspapers have been women. Perhaps this reveals the gendered categorization.

It's not a surprise that readers and reviewers, who are people of color or children of immigrants, critique the book on a deeper, more personal and insightful level. Moreover, there are nuances, psychological and cultural, that are more easily understood by readers of an East Asian immigrant background. Overall, though, I'm impressed and grateful that readers today seem generally more receptive and thoughtful about explicit discussions of race and the Asian-American experience, compared to when my first book was published in 2007.

Concerning the difference in how my two books were received, it's important to note that my first was marketed as general/literary fiction (when multiculturalism was the buzzword and the backlash was apparent in the reader reviews) while *Folklorn* was marketed toward the genre-reading community, which has become more and more politically progressive and diverse in the last decade or so. Thus, I can't help but wonder if *Folklorn* has been generously received because the "genre-reading" audience includes many who are progressive, adventurous, and more open-minded in their tastes, and if, because of their reading, they are more skilled in imagining and empathizing with the experiences and worlds of others from very different backgrounds. "Likability" among genre readers still seems to be a contentious issue, especially in regards to complex female protagonists. But maybe "relatability" of characters is more commercially influential/important among readers of realism?

It seems to me that many genre readers today are receptive and adventurous because their reading tastes require a nimble imagination and ease in absorbing unfamiliar worldbuilding, as well as alternative interpretations of history or speculations upon the future. Perhaps such readers aren't limited so much by "relatability" or "likability" as readers of realistic mainstream fiction are purported to be. Genre literature in the US these days seems much more politically progressive and diverse compared to mainstream literary publishing, but this is only my casual observation as a newcomer to the "genre community." Of course, there also seems to be a divide between "genre literature" that is described as "commercial" or "derivative/formulaic" and those books that are "literary," which might mean language-focused, character- or theme-driven, or experimental. (My observations, however, are filtered through my very limited social media exposure and the particular reviewers and publications I read.) Everything lies on a spectrum, of course, but dichotomies are easier to argue about on Twitter.

Did you encounter any discrimination specifically related to your gender in your writing career?
I'm sure I have, but racism eclipses gender discrimination. It's intertwined certainly, and I'm sure there are echoing sentiments and assumptions. There's also a sense of doubling the insult—for example, if after whatever achievement (getting an agent, winning a fellowship, getting published) I'm accused of benefiting because I'm a woman, it's because I'm a woman *and* an ethnic minority. Or, if my writing is dismissed as "woman's writing," there are the added limitations placed on it with the qualifier "Asian women's writing,"

etc. I've read plenty of novels by white women who write white male protagonists and are praised for not writing "women's fiction." I'm guessing that a novel of a white man written by an Asian woman or Black woman, however, would be less readily received. Too many border crossings, perhaps.

Generally speaking, in writing communities among students and professionals and in the publishing industry, there has long been an assumption that an explicitly "Asian-American book" was mainly autobiographical, unoriginal in style or structure, slotted into "immigrant fiction" with an expected, well-known narrative in the mode of trauma fiction. Nothing daring or original or ambitious. It might sell well and be appreciated in the publishing industry because it's "diverse" and "exotic." Unsurprisingly, many of my Asian women writer friends as students wrote white protagonists only, mostly male. None of these projects became published books, however, but they felt they were aiming for "literary fiction" or they wanted to be taken seriously, and not just be pigeonholed as an "Asian writer writing Asian stuff." Internalized racism. I'd be mocked or teased for writing solely about Koreans by both Asian and white friends. I'm forty-two years old. I wonder if it's different for young Asian writers today?

This was the assumption surrounding me as a student and an emerging writer, even by those who meant it encouragingly, as if to embrace this kind of book as a goal. It's as if "the Asian-American novel" was a readily reproducible genre in itself, a literary version of "they all look alike." In competitive writing programs or communities, there simmers a condescension and dismissal of "Asian-American stories" as being the same, already known, not artistic or original. Or more broadly, whatever writing award or achievement I got was because I was a minority or a woman. Or that being "ethnic" would serve as an advantage in publishing.

This is largely the reason why I've experimented with different stylistic modes in *Folklorn* and why I've enjoyed playing with genre tropes and tones. It allows me to flex prose muscles and challenge what readers assume of Asian-American fiction. In the past few years, there's been an explosion of Asian-American-authored books that are exhilarating in their experimentation, style, and subject matter. I was also thrilled to learn that the genre community includes many successful and respected Asian-American women authors.

There is today an ongoing debate around the word "genre" in the science fiction/horror milieu. Some agree with Ursula K. Le Guin that it is socially prejudiced; others claim that it is an essential and necessary literary "identity." As you have chosen to write a novel which uses the tropes of ghost stories and Korean folktales, what is your position on the subject?

I'm a writer coming from outside the "genre community" as a student, reader, and writer (or as my editor often points out, I'm coming from the literary fiction community). So yes, I will attest that there still exists a very generalized literary prejudice toward "genre fiction." However, in the last decade, I've observed a noticeable embrace of "genre elements" by writers considered "literary."

Often enough, I see that those in the "genre community" feel slighted when mainstream critics describe such works as "elevating genre" or touting plots and premises that are heralded as original and groundbreaking, when to "genre readers" these ideas are common and classic or overused tropes.

For my own interests as a writer and reader, I'm thrilled by the increasing intermingling of the two and most excited by writers of color who use genre elements, styles, structures to examine race, gender, and class in the US. I include the genres of thrillers and mysteries and romance in this broadening of literature.

It seems that the literary vs. genre argument erupts regularly on Twitter and in MFA grad programs, and I'm both bored and fascinated by it. Bored when the same old prejudices are repeated, but fascinated when I hear a new insightful take. Carmen Maria Machado and Kelly Link have spoken about this so-called divide, and I agree with Machado who says that there isn't so much a distinction between the literatures, but there is one between the reading communities. Kelly Link in an interview noticed this divide among her friends as well (I hope I'm remembering this correctly). But the judgment goes the other way, too. Both Kelly Link and Karen Joy Fowler have discussed how their early submissions to genre editors would be deemed as too literary for their publications, etc. This was early in their careers, and I believe these days there's a lot more overlap in journals and publishing house catalogs.

I often hear that it's more useful to discuss "genre" as a marketing industry term. *That* can certainly affect media coverage, awards consideration, and bookstore promotion. My agent and I never pitched myself as a genre writer or *Folklorn* as fantasy. But it was published by a "genre publisher" and promoted as "fantasy." Also very important, Erewhon's publicist/marketing manager, my editor, and the Erewhon founder are *all* firmly entrenched in the "genre community." My agent wanted my book to be presented as literary with genre elements in order to reach a wider readership. Erewhon was cooperative, but other forces took over as the algorithm on Amazon and Goodreads categorized *Folklorn* with books that were more fantasy-heavy or supernatural (because of the book description?). Many disappointed reviews from early readers/ bloggers debated its categorization, complaining there wasn't enough magic or supernatural elements to be fantasy, and that they were expecting a different kind of book. Yet because it was marketed as fantasy, others on Goodreads kept ticking that box for its category.

Admittedly, it's been a surprise that my book has been labeled as fantasy, but it's certainly benefited greatly from this and I'm grateful for the generosity of the genre community. I've had the wonderful luck of *Folklorn* being covered by mainstream publications, too. This all has more to do with marketing labels, blurbs, and positioning as well as the publicist's social network and my own circle of mentors, classmates, and friends. Social media is a much bigger influence on marketing and genre categorization today. Publishing my debut novel over fifteen years ago was nothing like my experience with *Folklorn*.

The term I always felt most appropriate for my work was "fantastical" and "gothic," though nobody else seems to agree about the gothic part. Perhaps your description of it being psychological horror most closely aligns with its gothic inspirations.

I've loved literary fiction that embraces the fantastical and the surreal ever since I started out as a student writer. At that time, I assumed, as an outsider, that genre pertained to hard science fiction or high fantasy. I didn't know it was as expansive and all-encompassing as I now know it to be. I think a lot of the social prejudice comes from others also assuming the same.

I agree with how some describe "literary" as a style, so that a genre novel might be written in a more literary style (character-driven, interior, and thematic) rather than plot-driven. Of course, a genre novel could be all things—literary in style *and* plot-driven *and* widely accessible *and* commercially successful. Using "genre" to describe such a wealth of diverse books is insufficient and potentially misleading, so it really depends on with whom we use the term and in which context. A bookseller told me that if they want to sell more of a fantasy or science fiction title, they need to include the word "literary" somewhere in the book description.

What was the determinant factor in your choice of this genre?
Writing in the modes of the fantastic, gothic, horror, surreal allows me to play with an expansive range of tones, colors, moods. I love to switch up tones unexpectedly and love creating atmosphere through language. The tragi-comic tone is served well by an overall heightened style in language and tone. This then tips easily into the surreal, the gothic, folkloric, supernatural, and hallucinatory. I love to plumb the psychology of a character, and using genre allows me to externalize the psychology and play with language and setting. Metaphors become literalized and something tangible to wrestle with or embrace, hide from or confront. I'm a maximalist as a writer and stylist, and thus a multigenre approach is how I write most freely.

What writers have you been influenced by? Was their gender important to you?
As a young student writer, my influences included Marguerite Duras, Colette, and—like any other young writer—Nabokov, Dostoyevsky, Bulgakov, etc. But this is embarrassing to admit and simply conveys my earnest youthful ambitions.

In and after grad school, my influences expanded to include Bruno Schulz and Isaac Babel and more contemporary writers: Aimee Bender, Lorrie Moore, Denis Johnson, Kevin Brockmeier, Kelly Link, Karen Joy Fowler, Helen Oyeyemi, Shirley Jackson, and Rachel Ingalls.

Gender was certainly important as well as a position of otherness and marginalization. In my early years as a writer, I didn't read much fantastic literature, but the Eastern European and French women writers I was drawn to evoke an emotional intensity in their prose that heightened the everyday reality of their scenes and character interactions and the very world they described. Like so many American university students who dream of writing, I was drawn to the Russian masters. The heightened tenor in describing internal and external states in such works led me one step toward an expressionistic writing style. I eventually took a step further by making the metaphor or image literal. The more restrained minimalist realism never appealed to me and seemed more foreign, culturally and aesthetically. What's most distinctly American in my writing is my voice and the hybridized, code-switching use of language or mixed tonal registers.

I found many contemporary American women writers to admire and learn from, who even if "realist," conveyed a heightened, othered perspective that reveals itself in absurdity, humor, the strange and tonally adventurous, like Lorrie Moore.

As a student, I read a lot of Asian-American literature and plenty of Kawabata and Murakami, but I felt more aesthetically and spiritually aligned with work by Black American writers. In the last several years, however, a new generation of brilliant Korean translators who are also English fiction writers have translated several Korean women writers who thrill me and overwhelm me with their power. These women have had long careers in Korea, but are now "introduced" to English readers through these translators. These women, many of whom write in the surreal, gothic, uncanny, fantastical, or mythic, could've been my influences, if I were able to read Korean literature. Relatedly, I've been greatly influenced by Korean films all my life. My elementary, familial comprehension of the Korean language and English subtitles, of course, made such films accessible to me. Korean films were definitely an influence in my use of the tragi-comic and the absurd/pathos.

More recently, my influences tend to be Black American speculative authors such as Mat Johnson and Victor LaValle and Octavia Butler.

What do you think renders horror genres apt to engage in identity and sexual politics?
A perfect segue! The Black American authors I list above utilize the absurd, horror, speculation, and fantasy in their interrogation and examination of America, including its history which is extremely horrific and rooted in human monstrosity. This history haunts all Americans today and poisons its future. But history and facts are easily forgotten or minimized. Films and literature that use horror genre tropes and structures make the reader feel, confront, and engage with race and sexuality, class and history. Horror penetrates beyond the factual and utilizes body horror, which emphasizes so

much about ownership, torture, commodification, control, etc. Horror uses the ghost story, hauntings, curses which can make the true horror more accessible or easier to contend with. If done effectively, the metaphor reaches into the reader and becomes more real, more resonant. There's a flexibility in the metaphors of horror for both the writer and the reader, who might be able to control how deeply they engage with the truth and history behind the horror metaphors.

In writing about my family's trauma through a fantastical lens, I was also able to control how deeply I'd confront certain memories. I could retreat emotionally by focusing on the story mechanics, the effectiveness of tropes, the imagery I enjoyed conjuring through words.

(I know I haven't *directly* answered the specifics of how the horror genre relates to identity and sexual politics. But I think my answer above is still relevant and resonant, though tangential or adjacent to your original question?)

Do you write with a gendered audience in mind?
I suppose I do. I'd hope Asian-American men would engage with the brother character and would feel I wrote about this character's experience with compassion. Though the book seems centered on women, I was very much aware of how an Asian-American man might read my novel and hoped to show a very complicated, nuanced depiction of the father and brother characters.

Do you think that horror and fantasy works are differently structured when addressed to traditionally under-portrayed individuals or communities?
I notice that books and films that focus on under-portrayed communities might need to lean on more common narrative tropes in order to make the story and characters more accessible, comprehensible to a mainstream readership or audience. (Or even get financed or published.) Sometimes, familiar genre structure or tropes can help the reader/viewer follow along despite the unfamiliar nuances of a different culture or racial perspective or a lesser-known history. Some works, however, seem to cater too much to be "familiar" and accessible, and thus the cultural, racial, or historical nods seem more like background setting, costume details, or ethnic

flavor. Contrasting to these might be books or films that embrace narrative rhythms or structures that aren't at all familiar to a mainstream audience or don't explain every single thing that's outside the dominant culture, or are willing to lose a reader unwilling to do more work to engage with the text.

In the books I've read that are addressed to or explore the experiences of marginalized communities through the horror or fantasy lens (Mat Johnson, Victor LaValle, Octavia Butler), I've noticed that more traditional narrative structures are used to initially draw in the reader and lull them with familiarity. But soon after, the structure becomes more complicated, overturned, or flipped inside out, or collapses into itself as if in interrogation of the dominant traditional structure and POV (point of view). This dismantling or deconstruction serves as the nightmarish revelation of the true, underlying horrors. As if the metaphor is ripped away to reveal the history or politics that still haunt and trap us today.

Is the portrayal of a minority specifically addressed to those that feel portrayed in these works?
Yes.

Your novel borders on psychological horror in order to question the notion of transnational and national identities. The main character of *Folklorn*, Elsa, is both haunted by the ghost of a girl and the painful memories linked to her mother. The feminine aspect seems to be linked with suffering, sacrifice, and remorse. Do you feel that you wanted to express a cultural specificity attached to Korean culture, or do you have a larger aim?
Through Elsa's examination of folklore, she is interrogating Korean notions of ideal femininity. But this Korean characterization of womanhood is then complicated by the mother who is more than a silent martyr and noble sacrifice. Elsa as an American who at times overcompensates to not seem like a stereotypical passive, meek Asian woman, grapples with the folklore and her mother's retellings to form her own understanding of what it means to be a Korean woman. Certainly, for me, my retellings are an attempt to show the revisionist, feminist truth underlying a lot of the sanitized tales. It's an attempt to show the rage and inequities that the folkloric women must've felt even if their stories don't reveal that. Revisionism in fairy tales and folklore is commonplace when it comes to European

tales, but Asian folklore is often still presented as exotic, quaint,
and a beautiful fantasy in many books published in the US. What's
been most surprising to me is how many woman readers who are
not Asian have identified with the mother–daughter relationship or
recognize the father character in their own families. Though my aim
was to examine Korean notions of femininity, the family dynamics
are more transnational than I'd realized.

**Do you feel that the ghost story genre offered you a possibility for
a transnational narrative, as these types of stories exist all over the
world?**
Yes. Also seems an apt and useful metaphor when writing from a
diaspora perspective, haunted by war and migration, memory and
history.

**As a writer with a Korean background, an American education, and
now living in Sweden, do you feel that gender borders exist? Or, as
in your novel, do identities just "go through" cultural realities like
neutrinos and antineutrinos do with matter?**
Of course, gender borders exist, further complicated by race and
class and nationality and education. Sometimes intertwined,
sometimes one subsumes the other. And just as one's status as a
racial minority might change in different contexts, cities, countries,
so does one's gender privileges and marginalization.

CHAPTER FIFTEEN

Jane Mondrup

Jane Mondrup (born in 1977) is a Danish steampunk and speculative fiction writer. Notable works: *Zeitgeist* (novel, 2019).

Dear Jane Mondrup, thank you very much for accepting to answer these few questions. This book is going to focus specifically on the notions of "gender" and "genre" as we believe that both are equally intersectional and are either confronted by or confronting territorial positions of dominance. In this light, can you tell us about your background and how this, in your eyes, influenced the person and the writer you are today?

I was born a total nerd in a very nerdy family of academics, teachers, and artists. Both my parents had degrees in music combined with history and literature, respectively, though my father later went on to become a computer programmer. They had been part of the 1970s progressive socialist movement, so feminist ideas were a core part of my upbringing.

I started reading at an early age and immediately went for the fantastic genres, beginning with fairy tales and moving on to fantasy and science fiction. My parents also read to me every night throughout my childhood, and they often chose adult books, which contributed to a certain fearlessness in my own reading. I wouldn't worry that something was beyond my level. I would just read it and understand whatever I could.

Apart from books I loved comics. We had a good collection at home, mostly children's comics like Asterix, Lucky Luke, and Spirou, but also more advanced stories like Valérian and Laureline, which you mention later. I would bring home piles and piles from the local library of both comics and books, sucking first the children's and then the adult's sections dry of anything that seemed interesting—which was mostly, but not exclusively, fantastic fiction of some kind or other.

During my high school years, I turned to punk and left-wing activism. This was really also a way of being a nerd, at least to me. I had always felt different, and now I flag it instead of trying to hide it. Then, I went on to study archaeology and history with a special interest in experimental archaeology and crafts, and though I wasn't employed within the field for very long, it probably shows quite clearly in my writing along with all the rest.

What do you think of women's position in science fiction today? Do you feel or have you felt any gendered resistance in the milieu or in the reviews?
There is no question that things have changed dramatically. When I grew up, female writers would be an exception, especially in science fiction. Now, not only women, but people with all kinds of gender and sexual identities have become a much bigger part of the writing community. To me it seems that the resistance to that is, if not exactly gone, then definitely waning—but how true that is, if you look outside the part of the milieu that I keep up with, I cannot say.

Did you encounter any discrimination specifically related to your gender in your writing career?
Not that I know of. But a recent survey of book reviews in Danish newspapers shows that female writers are much less likely to get reviews, and when they get them, they tend to be harsher. When my novel came out, I got two newspaper reviews. One of them was quite good, while the other was pure slating. Would that have been different if I were a man? I have no way of knowing, and I doubt it does me any good to ponder over it.

There is today an ongoing debate around the word "genre" in the science fiction/horror milieu. Some agree with Ursula K. Le Guin that it is socially prejudiced; others claim that it is an essential and necessary literary "identity." What is your position on the subject?
Though Le Guin talked about prejudice, she also took pride in being a science fiction writer, in contrast to Margaret Atwood who

has been quite dismissive of the term, preferring to call her own books speculative fiction. Though I actually quite like that term, I see absolutely no reason not to call Atwood's *The MaddAddam trilogy* (which I love) science fiction. Not only is it set in the future, but science plays a huge part in the story. The only reason to avoid labeling it science fiction is if you define the term qualitatively, as Atwood seems to do—if it's good, it's not science fiction (or fantasy, or horror).

I'm ferociously in the take-pride-in-your-genre camp, though at the same time I'm not especially respectful of genre boundaries. I write what I write. I'm very happy to call it science fiction, horror, fantasy, or whatever genre that seems to fit more or less, but I don't feel obligated to adhere to any rules. To the extent such rules exist, I'm sure they are more like guidelines. Sometimes you will choose to keep them, sometimes not. The important thing is if the book works within its own terms.

What authors have influenced your work? Why do you consider them important to you?
If we look at it chronologically my first big influence is the German author Michael Ende. His children's books *The Neverending Story* and *Momo* made a huge impression on me when I read them as a child, and as a teenager I found his surrealist stories. Together with the Danish author Svend Åge Madsen, whose stories also have surrealist aspects, he was the main influence on my earliest writing, at the age of fourteen to sixteen. I should probably also mention Douglas Adams here, but though I still love his books, especially the two about Dirk Gently, this influence didn't really carry over into my adult writing. A bit later I discovered Neil Gaiman who definitely became a lasting influence, especially his way of using mythology.

I had a writer's block all through my twenties, and though I read many good books in that period, I'm not sure how much they influenced me as a writer. I will mention one writer, though, that I read in that period: Kurt Vonnegut. I really admire his uncompromising storytelling. The way he wrote pleased absolutely nobody at the time, but it stands out in posterity as something really special.

When I started writing again around the age of thirty, my main, immediate influence was Susanna Clarke's debut novel *Jonathan Strange and Mr. Norrell*. There is a lot of Clarke in my own first novel, which I, after a few rejections, have kept in the trunk, exactly because I don't think it's independent enough. In contrast, I can't really name any obvious influences for *Zeitgeist*. Some elements were definitely borrowed from other works, and of course it reflects things I have read, but in a much more compilatory way.

In later years, I have started reading more short stories and have been immensely impressed by some dedicated short-story writers, from classics like James Tiptree, Jr. (= Alice Sheldon), over contemporary masters like Ted Chiang to a debutante like Veronica Schanoes. Tiptree's stories are unpleasant, but extremely compelling. Ted Chiang has a quiet intensity that I really admire, and Schanoes is twisting fairy tales into social realism, in a way that I at least haven't seen before.

I have also discovered Octavia Butler's very hard, but also moving and wonderfully vivid storytelling, and rediscovered Le Guin, whom of course I had read before, but not in depth. She was a pioneer in so many ways. Recently, I have developed an interest in the more subtle and poetic kind of horror stories which many of the other contributors to this book, such as **Priya Sharma, Penny Jones,** and **J. S. Breukelaar,** write. It's a style I also find in the magazine *Uncanny* which I have become a real fan of, and by which I'm definitely influenced in what I'm writing now.

Do you feel that science fiction has been influenced by the gender question? Is it the same for Danish science fiction?
Internationally, science fiction is definitely taking up all kinds of gender questions. In Denmark, gender topics have mainly reached the fantasy genre, at least as far as I know, but that's probably mostly because so little science fiction is actually published here. In the communities that I attend it is definitely part of the discussion, so I'm sure we will catch up.

How do you manage to negotiate the tension between stereotypical characters and worlds attached to specific genres in respect to gender images?
I'm very conscious about gender stereotypes, and I have always tried to either avoid them or twist them. What I haven't always done is think about the number of male characters contra other genders. While I was writing my first (trunk) novel, I came across the Bechdel Test, and I was horrified to discover that my story

completely failed it! Reflecting on how it had turned out that way I realized how male-centered most of the books I had read actually were. It was something I never thought about as a child, and funnily enough neither as a young person, despite my strong opinions on gender equality. It may have played a role that I never had a very strong gender identity, so I would identify with the male characters as easily as with the female, especially if they were somewhat nerdy.

Since then, I have been much more aware of my use of gender and of representation in a broader sense. This, of course, isn't just about the number of characters with a certain trait. The crucial thing is to make all of them life-like with their own personality, wishes, and ambitions. Too many female characters are mainly objects for the male protagonist's desire, and minority characters can easily end up as an instrument for somebody else's personal development. I do my best to steer clear of that, but I also try to avoid "positive" stereotypes—female or minority characters being ideals rather than people, with no negative characteristics. Every kind of character has the right to have weaknesses, quirks, or unpleasant qualities.

Do you write with a gendered audience in mind?

Not a specifically gendered audience, but definitely not an unspecified-and-therefore-male audience either. If anything, I write with a difference in mind. Not that I try to please everybody, but if you are interested in the same kind of things that I am, you should be able to read my stories and feel that I take all characters in them seriously.

Your novel, *Zeitgeist*, is a blend of fantasy, steampunk, and science fiction. What is determinant in your choice of these genres?

The story actually started as a role-playing game which I wrote back in 2010. We decided that it should be this new thing called steampunk, though we didn't really know what that was. So, we piled together a number of references which we considered kind of steampunky, and I started writing from there. The result probably had very little to do with actual steampunk, though in a live-action roleplay (LARP) it's very easy to add some hats, goggles, and copper color spray—and *voilà*!

Apart from the genre, my only starting point was something about Leonardo da Vinci and a Renaissance time machine. From there my mind started working in ways I cannot reconstruct, drawing in all kinds of scientific, mythological, philosophical, and historical elements to make a complete mash. I have no idea how I ended up with a nuclear disaster in the sixteenth century, for example, and it gave me no end of trouble later on. But it's a defining part of the story and I just had to work with it.

Then I started writing a novel based on the game and things just got even more complicated. It's actually very difficult for me to talk to about the book, exactly because it doesn't have a clear genre. Reviewers have suggested some I hadn't even thought about, such as retro futurism or dieselpunk. I'm happy with it all, as long as it doesn't give readers any expectations that the book doesn't fulfill.

As your novel takes place in a parallel past on Earth, and more specifically in the mid-1800s in Scandinavia (rebaptized "Scadinavia" in the story), did you think about women's place in society at the time? Was it a problem for you to create powerful female characters in a setting where sexist traditions were strong?
Not really. First, it's alternative history, so the world is as I make it, and second, all stories in any setting will have ample room for strong female characters. Even when women were the most oppressed, they had still played important roles in society. Some have fought their way across boundaries, others have had to stay within them and struggle quietly within rough and unfair circumstances—which takes an enormous amount of courage and stamina.

I gave myself some extra opportunities—for example, by making the Technician's Guild fully open to women. But sexism does exist and is addressed in the story. Some characters, such as countess Ildiko Hadik and the sisters of the Pandora Order, directly react against it, in ways I find completely understandable, though maybe not exactly positive.

A friend of mine once remarked that there are a lot of female villains in *Zeitgeist*. I don't really see them that way (with the possible exception of Gerda Stuckenbrock), but if we call them antagonists and also take into consideration that most of my characters are more or less ambiguous, then I guess you could say it's true —and the reason for it may be that you have more freedom with antagonists. You can explore all kinds of traits, also the ones very alien to you. I have done that in both male and female characters, but the female ones are definitely prominent.

(About Scadinavia: It was called that originally, back from Pliny the Elder. How the extra *n* sneaked its way in is not completely clear. I just took it out again.)

One of your main female character's names is Laureline, which is a tribute to the French science fiction comics *Valérian et Laureline* created by Pierre Christin and Jean-Pierre Mézières in 1967. Did you choose this name because of your love for the comics, or as a way to carry on the feminist aspect that Laureline impersonated at the time? And could it be seen as a sort of "genre crossover" between literature and comics?

Valérian et Laureline was one of the works I had in mind from the start when I wrote the original role-playing game. The main thing I took from it was the idea of the future changing the past and vice versa, as it happens in the duology *The Ghosts of Inverloch* and *The Wrath of Hypsis*, which to me personally is the true end of the series.

The reference wouldn't be obvious to a Dane, as Laureline is called Linda in the Danish translations, so the name was meant as a little tidbit for those who would catch it (there are others, more subtle, which I don't think anybody noticed yet). But I also really liked Laureline's character in the comics—though not as much in the later issues where she turns into more of a sex symbol. My Laureline has of course grown her own personality, and she is not in all aspects like her namesake. When it comes to jealousy and sexual relations, things are actually almost reversed.

Though it wasn't consciously for feminist reasons that I chose to include a character called Laureline, it can certainly be seen as a homage to the spirited, no-nonsense space-time agent that I remember from my childhood.

CHAPTER SIXTEEN

Lisa Morton

Lisa Morton (born in 1958) is an award-winning American horror writer and screenplay writer. Notable works: *The Castle of Los Angeles* (novel, 2010), *Night Terror & Other Tales* (collection, 2020).

Dear Lisa Morton, thank you very much for accepting to be part of this volume, which focuses specifically on the notions of "gender" and "genre" as we believe that both are equally intersectional and are either confronted by or confronting territorial positions of dominance. In this light, can you tell us about your background and how this, in your eyes, influenced the person and the writer you are today?
I had a childhood that I didn't realize was somewhat unique until well into middle age. My dad was a mad genius engineer who worked on everything from the helmets for NASA's Mercury space flights to the earliest PC motherboards, so I grew up playing with early tech; we also moved frequently because of his work, so I rarely had time to make friends in any place, which meant I entertained myself by making up stories. However, two other things were equally important: one was that Dad was also obsessed with hunting and fishing, so my mom and I would often be sitting in a freezing cold camper in the middle of nowhere while Dad was outside skinning a deer, meaning blood was something I got used to from a young age; and we were always in California (we spent one year in Northern California, but the rest of my life has been spent in Southern California), and living in this wonderfully diverse area

has absolutely shaped me. In fact, if I think of defining myself, geography is just as important to me as gender and genre.

Do you think women in horror are in a better position today than they were in the past centuries? Do you feel any gendered resistance in the milieu or in the reviews?
Women in horror are in a better position today than they were thirty years ago, when I was first breaking into the genre. Back in the 1980s and early 90s, there were very few well-known women horror writers—Anne Rice, of course, and a handful of others, but not many; you could go down the table of contents on nearly any anthology or magazine and find one or no female names. Now, there are so many wonderful writers who identify as female!

However, having now co-edited (with Leslie Klinger) two volumes of *Weird Women: Classic Supernatural Fiction by Groundbreaking Female Writers*, I've come to realize that women writing horror in the nineteenth century actually had some interesting advantages: although it's true that they often had to publish under their married names, initials, or anonymously, there were a surprising number of them, and they could make a living—enough, even, to support a family—writing primarily short fiction. Genre was not a restraint for them, because they almost all moved freely between different types of writing—Elizabeth Gaskell, for instance, who wrote the classic ghost story, "The Old Nurse's Story," is equally well known for her novels of social commentary.

Did you encounter any discrimination specifically related to your gender in your writing career?
I started my career as a screenwriter, and yes, in that area of writing I absolutely did, including one agent who was more interested in setting me up for dates with his older male clients than actually selling my work. As a prose writer in the field of horror, I can't say that I've encountered any obvious discrimination . . . but I also can't say with certainty that I've experienced *no* discrimination.

There is today an ongoing debate around the word "genre" in the science fiction/horror milieu. Some agree with Ursula K. Le Guin that it is socially prejudiced; others claim that it is an essential and necessary literary "identity." What is your position on the subject?

That's an interesting question. Horror certainly hasn't always had the finest reputation, but neither have the other genres. Genre is a useful marketing concept, but it is also constricting to both readers and writers; I know that as I've aged, I've become more interested in writing material that doesn't fit easily into a single genre . . . and yes, those pieces can be more of a challenge to sell.

Overall, I'm happy to be labeled a horror writer because it's a genre I've loved my entire life and that is host to so many fine authors, but it does carry the risk of curtailing some opportunities.

How did you choose to write horror? Was it a conscious decision?
No—to quote Lady Gaga, I was born this way. It was what I loved from a very young age (and I was fortunate that both my parents thought a toddler obsessed with monster movies was adorable). I don't think I realized I wanted to write it (horror) for a vocation, however, until I saw *The Exorcist* during its initial release. It's hard to get younger people now to understand what enormous power that movie had over its audiences; I was fifteen when I saw it in a packed theater, and to be surrounded by people who were shaking and screaming and fleeing the theater and fainting . . . well, I realized that I wanted to be able to affect people that way with art. I went into that theater wanting to be an anthropologist; I came out wanting to be a horror writer.

What writers have you been influenced by? Was their gender important to you?
Growing up, I was most influenced by Bradbury, Sturgeon, Lovecraft, Ellison, and (later) Dick, so no—the writer's gender wasn't important to me. However, my favorite books and stories (especially Frank Herbert's *Dune*) were often the ones that featured strong female protagonists.

What renders horror genres apt to engage in sexual politics?
Horror deals head-on with our fears of being vulnerable, and unfortunately that has often been translated into horror stories about women as victims. I once did a blog post back in the mid-90s in which I mentioned that I'd just read something like eight horror books in a row that included rape scenes; this was during a cycle in which horror movies tended to feature scenes of rape and torture, and that was reflected in the prose. Horror, I think more than any other genre,

tends to feed off its cinematic side, so if the current movies are expressing a particular trend, the literature will pick that up.

I actually wish more horror would engage more directly with sexual politics. I always find it ironic that many horror writers avoid anything like that for fear of being "preachy"; horror is one genre that should never be risk-averse!

How are these genres modified in order to accommodate contemporary post-identitarian claims?
The most obvious answer to that is to make room for a more diverse slate of writers. For far too long all of the genres have been dominated by white male writers, so much of the literature had a certain sameness to it. Organizations, like the Horror Writers Association, can help by emphasizing diversity and inclusion, and by creating opportunities for underrepresented writers. I served as President of the Horror Writers Association from 2014 to 2019, a time when so much of society was undergoing major cultural shifts in terms of identification and representation, and although it was sometimes difficult to navigate those shifts, I look back now and say that one of the things I'm proudest of having accomplished was the creation of new ways to recognize and assist more diverse writers. Every genre needs that fresh blood to progress.

In horror fiction, transgressive sexualities are meant to tame the uncanniness, to exorcise sexuality's threat to the self by weaving it into the trauma of horror. Did the enhancement of social acceptability recalibrate what startles, horrifies, or repulses either readers or characters?
I'd love to think so! But I think we're still in the middle of that recalibration. I look forward to that day when I don't have to watch a new horror movie and cringe at how women and people of color are set up to serve as victim fodder. For a pleasant change, the literature of horror is ahead of the cinema in this regard.

In "genre fiction" such as horror, fantasy, or science fiction, there seems to be a tension in character identity as well as plot structure and situations between recognizable stereotypes that characterize a genre and facilitate reading, and, on the other hand, the malleability of the imaginary allowed by the construction of alternative universes. How do you manage to negotiate this tension with respect to gender images?

I know that I, as a writer, take pleasure in occasionally calling out those stereotypes and destroying or inverting them, regardless of how they define a genre. Why, for example, shouldn't the victim be the strongest character, especially if the antagonist is supernatural? Why shouldn't a character who might be traditionally considered weak be elevated to hero status?

One of the reasons that I've always loved the work of Philip K. Dick is that his heroes are often of the working class; he really dispensed with tired notions of heroes who were supermen or who possessed extraordinary knowledge. That's something that I think is often the case with my work as well—my protagonists tend to be teachers, store clerks, or office workers thrust into horrific situations. One of horror's most overused tropes is the protagonist who is a writer, so that's certainly one I try to avoid.

The several subcategories that emerged with regard to horror (gay, lesbian, transgender, feminist, black, etc.), enhanced by the different anthologies that we can find in the market, not only signify the portrayal of specific identities or communities, but also each of them seems to address a specific audience. You have edited (with Leslie Klinger) an anthology of classical horror stories written by women. Did you edit it with a gendered audience in mind?
No! We wanted these overlooked writers to be enjoyed by as wide an audience as possible. When these women were first published, they often wrote under male pseudonyms (Vernon Lee, for example) or their stories were published anonymously, so readers didn't even know they were female. Although we wanted our modern readers to recognize the gender of these extraordinary women, we also believe the stories can be enjoyed by modern readers of any gender.

I also have to note that as a reader in the horror genre, I love exploring anthologies that may be themed around a community I'm not incredibly familiar with, and I'd like to think I'm not alone in that.

Do you think that horror works are differently structured when addressed to traditionally under-portrayed individuals or communities?
That's a hard question to answer at this point in the genre's evolution because works addressed to those individuals or communities are still relatively new and evolving. My gut instinct is to say that we all

share certain anxieties—the fear of death, of the unknown, of our own bodies, of what's out there beyond our understanding—so we ideally should all respond to a well-told story that may not center on our own community. I think of, for example, Gabino Iglesias's extraordinary book *Coyote Songs*, which employs those fears and drew widespread acclaim from audiences who were not the Latinx characters and immigrants depicted in the book; that book did employ an unconventional structure (it was somewhere between a novel and a collection), but I can also point to works like Jordan Peele's brilliant *Get Out* as a work targeted at a specific demographic that employs a classic horror structure and certain tropes.

Your novels, such as *The Castle of Los Angeles* and *Malediction*, feature strong female characters who dominate the stories, both as heroines and villains. Was that a voluntary choice to downplay the traditional male role in horror stories, or a desire to link your protagonists with the archetypal figures of the good and bad witch?
The flip answer is: That's just *me*. I'm female, and it just feels natural to me to focus on female characters. I'm always surprised by women writers who say they'd rather write male characters, because that's not been my experience at all.

In *The Castle of Los Angeles*, I couldn't help thinking that your Jessamine Constanza character who paints occult works is reminiscent of the somewhat scandalous Australian figure Rosaleen Norton, who was a very provocative figure of the 1950s, 60s, and 70s. How do you consider these kinds of feminine edge-figures and their role?
Oh, I don't know Rosaleen Norton, so now I have to go look her up (thank you!). Jessamine was actually based on some women I'd known and worked with, in particular a female producer I'd spent a considerable amount of time with and who, I suspect, thought she was somehow mentoring me (which is somewhat the dynamic Jessamine has with the protagonist Beth in the novel). In other words, I'd like to say that she was a creation who was deliberately exploring some sort of feminine archetype, but the reality is that she was me digging into personal experience.

You have also worked on nonfiction books about traditions and figures traditionally linked with horror such as Halloween, witches,

and spiritist seances where gender and genre actually historically play a big part. Should these books be seen as "statements" on your part, in a gender-oriented way?

I'd say "no" in regards to my Halloween history books, but I wouldn't be averse to having *Calling the Spirits: A History of Seances* read that way. So many of the "superstar" nineteenth-century mediums, including the Fox Sisters (who invented the seance) were female that gender simply *must* be discussed in a history of that practice. When you start reading the lives of these women—how many came from middle-class families that left them with few opportunities beyond the expected wife-and-mother route—you begin to understand how attractive mediumship must have looked for them. It's also interesting to note that the biggest male medium among the Victorian Spiritualists, Daniel Dunglas Home, may well have been gay, so again mediumship becomes a way to create opportunities that would not otherwise have existed for someone with that gender identity in that time and place. These mediums were performing for royalty and aristocracy, they were treated to extravagant gifts of money and property, and they were feted in Spiritualist newspapers and magazines (of which there were many), so it certainly would have looked like a way out of Victorian gender identity constraints. And by the way, lest that be read as a statement that these mediums were all knowingly engaging in fraud, let me note that I have no doubt many of them genuinely believed they possessed supernatural gifts, and it doesn't matter whether we share that belief or not.

CHAPTER SEVENTEEN

Malka Older

Malka Older (born in 1977) is an American speculative fiction writer and academic. Notable works: *Tear Tracks* (story, 2015), *Infomocracy* (novel, 2016).

Thank you very much for accepting to answer these few questions. Speculative fiction—and science fiction, in particular—has traditionally been regarded as a male-oriented genre. Before the advent of second-wave feminism and the gay liberation movement in the 1960s, women writers were denied recognition not as much by publishing houses as by science fiction nominations and awards. Do you feel this gender-oriented differentiation among genres still prevails today?
I think it still exists in some places and spaces. It's certainly not dominant among the people I mostly interact with, but it's still around to the extent that I occasionally glimpse the edges of it.

Have you personally felt any gendered resistance in the milieu or in the reviews?
I don't think so, but it's hard to be sure. Were there reviewers who would have been less critical of the "complexity" of my world if I were male, for example? Or would I have gotten more press in general? I can't know. But I don't think so, responses were generally positive to my books.

Did you encounter any discrimination specifically related to your gender in your writing career?

As above, I don't think so, but I can't be sure, I don't know what the counterfactual would be.

I did have an interesting gender-related moment when my first book, *Infomocracy*, was included in a Fathers' Day promotion from my publisher. I was (as far as I could tell) the only female author included. I hate Fathers' and Mothers' Day advertising in general already. I'm not sure why my book was included; it could have been a conscious attempt on the part of someone to include a female author; also, I happen to know that my editor had shared my book with their father and he had really liked it, so it could have been as simple as that. But it made me think about why my book might be perceived as "masculine" enough for Fathers' Day—data? Geopolitics? A thriller plot? Male point of view characters along with the female ones? I tried to appreciate the publicity and the subversion of the idea that men only read books by men, but I never felt entirely comfortable about it.

There is today an ongoing debate around the word "genre" in the science fiction/horror milieu. Some agree with Ursula K. Le Guin that it is socially prejudiced; others claim that it is an essential and necessary literary "identity." What is your position on the subject?
I have always read (and written) across a wide range of genres, and usually when I'm looking for something to read the genre trappings of it are less important to me than whether it's a good story, whether the characters are ones that I want to spend time with, and whether the mood of the book—intense, fun, suspenseful—fits my own. There are times when I feel drawn toward one genre over another, but it's rarer. So, while I recognize that genre can be a useful shorthand to tell us certain things about a book, I don't see it as an identity or essential. And what we choose to use as genre labels are, of course, socially constructed.

The 1960s and 70s are perhaps the most influential decades in the study of gender in speculative fiction. Not only was there an influx of female speculative fiction writers, but also many of these writers applied feminist theory to speculative fiction (Ursula K. Le Guin, Angela Carter, etc.). At the same time, the emergence of African-American female voices brought to light the intersectionality between gender and race. It is as if speculative fiction genres offered better than others the opportunity to challenge social conventions,

especially gender, and to explore alternative sexualities and alliances. Is it the case in your work? Have you been influenced by specific writers of this generation? Do you think that the speculative fiction genre is more apt to engage in sexual politics than mainstream literature?

Not really. As in other genres, there's a range. I think the Robert Heinlein book, *The Number of the Beast*, was the first time I read about homosexuality described very casually as an unsurprising aspect of human interaction; but then I read *Maurice*, which was of course written much earlier (and with different purpose, naturally). And I remember very clearly reading another Heinlein book, *The Star Beast*, which I loved as a kid, but also leans heavily on gender stereotypes in its female character. In my course, I teach *The Pushcart War* as a science fiction book: it is extraordinarily relevant on activism, collective action, power dynamics, political corruption, technology, but despite being written by a woman, it is very rooted in the gender roles of the 1950s, while some literary books, fantasy books, or non-science fiction kids' books written at the time were pushing harder. It varies.

Do you think that the position and struggles of women today require to structurally modify the invention of alternative worlds or utopian/dystopian futures?

I'm not sure I understand the question. Women (and everyone else, pretty much) would benefit hugely, if the power structures that determine what movies get made (and to a lesser but still important extent what books are published/sell) were less male, less white, and less focused on profit. I say particularly movies because our conception of sexualization as a marketing tactic is still heavily linked to the visual, and movies continue to be dominated by a male gaze that is unhelpful for artistic value, for entertainment value, and certainly for any realism in the depiction of gender or sexuality, and that strongly affects science fiction movies/TV shows as well, whether they're utopian or dystopian.

If you mean whether we need to restructure our conceptions of alternative worlds/futures to imagine different gender relations, always. We should always be imagining different permutations of society, whether as goals or warnings or just weirdness, because the flexibility and plasticity of our human interactions and cultures is a marvel that we should be imagining in as many different ways as possible.

In "genre fiction" such as fantasy, speculative fiction, and other formulaic genres, there seems to be a tension in character identity as well as plot structure and situations between recognizable stereotypes that characterize a genre and facilitate reading, and, on the other hand, the malleability of the imaginary allowed by the construction of alternative universes. How do you manage to negotiate this tension with respect to gender images?

I consciously try to break or subvert them. I don't always catch myself, but I try—and I appreciate when editors help by pointing out what I've missed, too.

The several subcategories that emerged with regard to speculative fiction (gay, lesbian, transgender, feminist, black, etc.), enhanced by the different anthologies that we can find in the market, not only signify the portrayal of specific identities or communities, but also each of them seems to address a specific audience. Do you write with a gendered audience in mind?

Most fundamentally, I write for myself, I write the books that I want to read. I do, however, try to keep in mind that I don't know who might be reading the books, that I want to reflect the world as it is and not erase certain people because they're not me. When I include people that I might have forgotten about because they're not often in media—pregnant women, nonbinary people, disabled people, just for example—I'm not writing that for those people. Pregnant women (to use an example) already know that they don't see themselves much in media, and that when they are it's usually in the service of stereotypes and without agency; yes, I hope they appreciate the representation, but I'm also writing pregnant women into my books for the people whose main experience with pregnant women is through those stereotypical portrayals. They're the ones who need to see such characters integrated into the story. And, again, I'm writing for myself, because I want books in which the cast of characters feels more like the random diversity you encounter in real life than the airbrushed, carefully selected cast of extras in a popular movie.

Your *Infomocracy* trilogy (*Infomocracy*, *Null States*, and *State Tectonics*) doesn't specifically tackle gender issues, and male and female characters are fairly evenly distributed in the novels. Was that a conscious choice on your part?

Initially, not so much. I was writing a cyberpunk-inspired global thriller, I needed lots of characters, I scattered them across genders. But when I came to writing the sequels, I decided that I wanted to make sure I was showing more different examples of women as heroic figures, and so I consciously chose to center a different woman in each subsequent book, and to make them different in abilities and character and concerns. Mishima is in many ways a typical action hero—not entirely so, as she's neuroatypical and perhaps has more interiority and self-doubt than most, but she's very physically competent and decisive and not risk-averse. Then we have Roz, who is really not about physical action, is more about personal interaction, and has a very different arc from Mishima; and then Maryam, who is more on the tech side and engages in a different kind of action.

One of your main female protagonists, Mishima, has a male reference to it (Yukio Mishima was a queer Japanese writer), while a male protagonist, Domaine, has a female-sounding appellation. Was that also intentional? And, if yes, what was your purpose with this?
Mmm, not super intentional. I was thinking about Yukio Mishima when I named Mishima, but that early on in the process. I am very much letting myself choose things as they come to mind, not trying to design too hard. Also note that while the final *e* makes Domaine seem like a feminine word in English, it is not so in French; and Mishima is a surname. Mainly, I was just looking for cool names.

Your short story "Tear Tracks" is a very beautiful story with a strong feminist message, turning around familiar womanhood tropes. What inspired you to write this story?
That story was inspired by a terrible thing that happened to someone I knew, and thinking about the courage their mother showed and how unappreciated, unvalued, that kind of courage and emotional depth is. The story is designed in an attempt to show readers what they're missing by accepting, unquestioned, our societal definitions of what makes people brave, or great, or leaders, or important. And that tends to be extremely gendered.

CHAPTER EIGHTEEN

Nuzo Onoh

Nuzo Onoh (born in 1962) is a British-Nigerian horror writer. Notable works: *The Sleepless* (novel, 2016), *A Dance for the Dead* (novel, 2022).

Dear Nuzo Onoh, thank you very much for accepting to be part of this volume, which will focus specifically on the notions of "gender" and "genre," two notions that often intersect in literature. In this light, can you tell us about your background and how this, in your eyes, influenced the person and the writer you are today?
Thank you, Seb. I grew up the third of eight children. My father was a British-trained lawyer, a politician and businessman. He was also a Protestant by religion, and the Chancellor of the Anglican Church. My mum was a retired headteacher and a devout Catholic. She had to give up her career once she married, as per the cultural norm for women married into affluent families at the time. She was also forced to give up her beloved Catholic religion, something she fought against throughout her turbulent marriage. She spent the rest of her life sneaking off to attend Mass and dealing with the violent fallout whenever my father or his relatives found out. My mother was also from a different village from my father's and for the entirety of her married life, she was considered a stranger by my father's people, who referred to her as "The woman from Eke Village." Her constant struggles to provide sons for my father resulted in the eight children she birthed, and I grew up knowing that my brothers, even the youngest one, were more valued than I was. I spent the rest of my youth rebelling against

this patriarchal structure and getting incessant corporal punishment for my actions.

The Biafran–Nigerian War (1967–70) was a baptism of fire for every Biafran child. We lived in the capital city, Enugu, and overnight my family and my people became refugees, abandoning everything to escape the Nigerian enemy bombs. My father became a colonel in the army and was absent from the various towns and villages we stayed in as war refugees. Death became a daily occurrence, and in time, the sight of rotting corpses by the wayside or en route the streams became quite normal. I remember watching screaming and wailing adults dragging out bodies from a bomb-hit bunker. Several of my relatives died in the course of the war.

Yet, despite the harrowing situation, the Biafran government ensured that we children always attended school. The school ground was where we were given food from the international relief agencies and taught patriotic anti-Nigeria and anti-Britain songs. The British government were the chief supporters of our enemies, and till date, every Biafran holds them as responsible as the Nigerians for the pogrom of our people. I believe that the education I received in those three years of civil conflict ensured that I didn't lag behind in my education after the war.

Every evening after school, we looked forward with great anticipation to the *Tales by Moonlight* sessions to distract and entertain us. These were usually ghost stories and folktales brimming with superstitions, supernatural vengeance, and triumph of good over evil. Sometimes, Christian religion contents encroached into the stories, albeit the ancestors and gods always played prominent roles in these fantastical tales. There was generally little supervision by adults, with the able-bodied men away fighting, while the women were preoccupied with providing for their children. As a result, we children saw and underwent unwholesome things, which all children in war zones experience. By the time the war finally ended and we were able to return to our ravaged towns and homes to start afresh, we had all become little adults, ready to take our uncertain place in society.

The war had a profound effect on gender roles, with many Biafran women taking on roles formerly reserved for the menfolk during the conflict. But in my family, it simply solidified the old system. My father became more chauvinistic and misogynistic after the war, creating an environment of fear and intimidation in the house. Eventually, he started sending out his kids to various English and Scottish Quaker boarding schools, a trend that was popular among affluent families burdened with a terrible colonial complex. And my siblings and I became what we are today, a hybrid of the two cultures.

From this brief account, anybody that has read my books would instantly understand the impact my childhood had on my writing. My stories are always about supernatural vengeance and occultic magic. They brim with superstitions, lore, and religious conflicts as they explore the good, the bad, and the ghastly of African culture within a horror context. They follow the strict gender roles of my upbringing and the women are always fighting to break free from the oppressive and patriarchal systems. And just as in our *Tales by Moonlight* stories, good generally trumps evil.

As a person, I believe I've become very resilient with a "can-do" attitude, coupled with a resistance to authoritarian figures, religious beliefs, and anything that would aim to curb my freedom. I have also become an extremely protective mother, a somewhat bad trait that has resulted in my two daughters literally running away from home and my city to establish their independence from my smothering tendencies. Thank heavens for mobile phones and social media, where I can troll them, lol.

Do you think women in horror and fantasy are in a better position today than when you began to write? Did you encounter any discrimination specifically related to your gender in your writing career?
I think things have definitely picked up for women in both the horror and fantasy genres. There are more female writers of both genres than ever before. Gone is the need to hide under a male pseudonym in order to be taken seriously as a writer of horror and fantasy. The Twitter horror community is a very supportive one that helps fellow writers to develop and grow. In my case, I was writing a unique horror subgenre, which didn't come with the baggage and restrictions of conventional horror writing. But it encountered its own unique discriminations, nonetheless. Many agents and publishers refused to touch my work. I got tired of receiving the same mantra, "Great story, but not sure how to market this one."' I had no similar or comparable works to direct them to, and Black Lives Matter hadn't happened at the time. I ended up publishing and marketing myself at great expense till I established my brand.

Do you feel Nigeria has a specific identity when it comes to women writers and genre?

Definitely, Nigerian female writers have driven the plethora of genre wagons for longer than I can recall. Women from my community especially. the Biafran-Igbo people, have always exhibited impressive dexterity in crafting literary and genre works. I grew up reading books by Flora Nwapa, known as the mother of modern African literature, Buchi Emecheta, and Ifeoma Okoye, three amazing writers and fellow Igbo women who inspired my young heart to nurture a dream that has thankfully come to fruition. P. A. Ogundipe (1927–2020) became the first Nigerian woman to be published in the English language in 1946, during the colonial era. Today, other Nigerian names, like Chimamanda Ngozi Adichie, Nnedi Okorafor, Helen Oyeyemi, and Adaobi Tricia Nwaubani to mention but a few, are now household names in their various genres. The writer Wole Talabi recently addressed the question of gender in African speculative fiction in his article, "Preliminary Observations from an Incomplete History of African SFF." He used statistics, charts, and graphs to show the impact African female writers of speculative works have had on the genre. His research showed that "almost 70% of science fiction works were by male authors, but under 50% for fantasy and horror." (https://www.sfwa.org/2022/06/01/preliminary-observations-incomplete-history-african-science-fiction-fantasy/)

Nigeria is the cradle of "Afrofuturism." Do you think there is also a Nigerian specificity of the "horror" genre? Could we talk of "Afrohorror" in the same way as for science fiction?

Thanks to the likes of Nnedi Okorafor, Oghenechovwe Donald Ekpeki, Wole Talabi, Tade Thompson, Tochi Onyebuchi, Suyi Davies Okungbowa, and a host of other Nigerian writers of the genre, speculative fiction works are no longer in the sole domain of the Western world. However, as the writer Nnedi Okorafor noted in her blog post, *Nnedi's Wahala Zone Blog* (http://nnedi.blogspot.com/2019/10/africanfuturism-defined.html), there is a difference between AfricanFuturism and Afrofuturism. Afrofuturism engages with both American and African cultures, while AfricanFuturism is rooted in the mother-soil and written predominantly by people of African descent both in Africa and the wider diaspora. So, despite other big African names in the genre like **Eugen Bacon** and

Tlotlo Tsamaase, for instance, this is a genre being driven in the main by Nigerian writers, with numerous awards, both locally and internationally, won in recognition of their talents. So, one can confidently claim that Nigeria is indeed the cradle of AfricanFuturism.

When it comes to horror, most people are aware that I pioneered the terminology "African Horror" with regard to works of speculative fiction. In my quest to change the phrase "African Horror" from the negative portrayal of the African continent by the popular Western media, I adopted it instead as a genre terminology to describe my horror stories. These days, it is now recognized as a bona fide regional horror genre, just like the Korean, Japanese, or Scandinavian horror works.

Like Nnedi Okorafor, I don't believe that my works, rooted deeply in African culture and beliefs, can be termed Afrohorror. It is little surprise, therefore, that I am mostly referred to as the queen of African horror, instead of the queen of Afrohorror. In my lecture at the Miskatonic Institute of Horror Studies in London, I mentioned the difference between African horror writers and other writers who write horror stories set in Africa, and explained the importance of authenticity in the narrative. African horror works must be rooted in the African world and culture for authenticity, just like every other regional work of horror.

Initially, the Nigerian Nollywood film industry dominated the horror narrative coming out of Nigeria. Writers of horror works either found their stories wrongly classified as multicultural works, African Literature, or other broad and limiting non-genre-specific classifications. As a result, there was no strong specificity of the written horror genre in Nigeria for a long time. Thankfully, things are now moving in a positive direction, albeit slowly. More Nigerian horror writers are getting their works rightly classified and marketed. The founding of the African Speculative Fiction Society, in 2016, has also strengthened the genre, especially with its NOMMO award for speculative fiction. However, fantasy works appear to be the dominant narrative, together with science fiction. Horror works from Nigeria are still rooted strongly in the short story/novella categories. There is, therefore, a strong need for longer works of horror by Nigerian writers, instead of the plethora of impressive and award-winning short stories and novellas currently making the rounds in the international horror circuits.

You write horror. What is determinant in your choice of this genre?

First, growing up listening to ghost stories during the nightly *Tales by Moonlight* sessions, mostly told by my late uncle Sebastian Afadi. Till date, nothing beats that delicious shiver of anticipation as I waited for my uncle to clear his throat loudly, give us a long, fierce look, before asking us if we were ready, if we were really, really, ready to hear his story. He slowly built the terror in our little hearts even before he said the first word or sang the first dirge linked to the tale. Secondly, the fantastical tales of transmogrifications and occult rituals I heard from my late mother, whom I always called the consummate storyteller, have influenced my choice of the horror genre. My books are riddled with the lore and superstitions I heard from my mother and uncle through my childhood and adulthood. Finally, the Brothers Grimm fairy tales I consumed as a child more or less sealed my preference for the horror genre.

What writers have you been influenced by? Was their gender important to you?

I must confess that in my less enlightened years, I always felt that male writers made better horror writers. This was due to the fact that my first introduction to the genre were stories written by men, The Brothers Grimm, later followed by Amos Tutuola. In addition, our *Tales by Moonlight* storytellers were always "Uncles." By the time I discovered Stephen King, I was completely ruined and totally indoctrinated. It finally took Ann Rice to break my prejudice and show me that women writers could be just as deadly as the men. These days, Tananarive Due, V. Castro, and Yoko Ogawa, among other modern female horror writers, have shown us that women horror authors are a force to be reckoned with. My early influences and their books I loved: Amos Tutuola (*The Palmwine Drinkard*), Cyprian Ekwensi (*Juju Rock*), Stephen King (*Cujo*), Ann Rice (*Interview with the Vampire*), Daphne du Maurier (*Don't Look Now*), and Steven Pressfield (*Gates of Fire*). This book, while not strictly horror, contains so much horror in every page that it stayed with me for life. Like *The Godfather*, I've read it at least thrice. It is so amazing in character development that I still refer to it whenever I need to give a nudge to any of my characters who are reluctant to reveal themselves fully to me.

Your main characters are sometimes male, sometimes female. What makes you choose one gender over the other in a story? Is this choice important for you?
My characters' gender is rarely ever my choice. I just go with whichever character wants me to tell their story. Sometimes, they are male voices I hear in my head; other times, female or children's voices. So, their gender is not something that is particularly important to me as I don't think it is my place to choose or select which character to portray. Basically, whenever the individual characters' voices become so insistent that I'm losing sleep fighting my laziness to tell their stories, I know it's finally time to go to my laptop and empty my mind.

In my interview with *Short Story Day Africa*, I made the following statement: "I never bother drawing up outlines for stories as my characters inevitably decide how they want to be portrayed and I just let myself be led by them. Can't recall the number of times I've read a story I'd written and wondered how it ended up that way. I'm sure lots of writers have had a similar experience. Makes you wonder if these characters we think we're creating as writers don't actually possess some distinct corporal existence somewhere with a living intelligence, powerful enough to influence our thoughts and fingers." (http://shortstorydayafrica.org/news/my-stories-are-mostly-themed-around-vengeance-an-interview-with-horror-writer-nuzo-onoh)

Do you write with a gendered audience in mind?
No. I think my characters will speak to whoever they wish, male or female. While I find that, for some reason, my fanbase is predominantly middle-aged male, I also have many female readers who connect with my characters. One can never tell for whom the story tolls.

Do you see yourself as a "women author" or as an "author"? Is your gender connected to your identity as a writer, or do you consider it as a secondary definition?
Most days, I simply see myself as a writer of African horror stories. I only remember my gender when I'm asked by some of my fellow middle-aged African women, why I choose to write such "demonic" works instead of something Christ would approve of. When Black

Lives Matter happened with all the awful revelations accompanying it, I also remembered that I was a black female writer in a white-dominated environment, whose career trajectory might have been different but for the structural racism of the industry.

Your audience is international, but you specifically write about Nigeria. Do you think the horror genre makes your culture more accessible to wider audiences?
The best thing that has happened with the horror genre is the emergence of regional horror across the globe. Horror fans, long jaded by more of the same coming from the West, are turning increasingly to stories from different cultures for their terror-fix. I've been told by many Western fans that they never had any idea about the Biafran War till they read my book *The Sleepless*. I remember how thrilled I was when I read Yoko Ogawa and Otsuichi and discovered Japanese horror for the first time; or when I watched *Train to Busan* and discovered Korean horror films. My greatest desire is for the market to be flooded with translated Korean horror novels and books from every culture in the world. It is therefore my humble hope that my readers experience the same thrill when they discover African horror through my books.

In your stories, family is often a central element of the narrative: children, parents, husbands, wives, or siblings are both the protagonists and often the victims. Do you feel that this choice of social setting is a gendered choice from your side, or are you simply using a basic and universal material?
I neither think about any choice of social setting nor a gendered consideration, when I write my stories. I think one good fortune we have as African writers when writing about our experiences is the ability to do so with neither conscious awareness nor attention to outside influences and foreign gazes, as may happen to black writers outside the continent, writing about their own prejudiced worlds and experiences. The days of Negritude are over for many African writers, especially writers from West Africa. We just write what is as it is. As mentioned, I tend to let my characters—male, female, and children—use me as their conduit and I try to tell their stories to the best of my abilities. I believe that it is through the intimate lenses of the characters and the family dynamics that we can authentically explore the bigger picture in the society, a picture that can be

horrible, tragic, haunting, harrowing, and, at times, even terribly beautiful.

In many occasions, children are sacrificed by evil witch doctors in your stories. In the West, we have a number of fairy tales based on the same themes. Do you think that the horror genre is a way for these myths to survive? And perhaps remain as warnings on the monstrosity of our human nature?

First of all, let us disabuse ourselves of the notion that child sacrifices in the West are only relegated to the realms of fairy tales. A perusal of news from around the world will reveal the prevalence of this odious practice across all cultures. In the West, many of these sacrifices are linked to ritualistic sex abuse of children. Secret cults and Satanic groups are said to be involved in this. We have the 2019 ritual killings of two children by their parents in Valencia, Spain, for instance. I always say that Dennis Wheatley's works did not happen in a vacuum. His stories of the occult and the ritualistic murders in Europe were not based on fairy tales. He was very close friends with the notorious occultist Aleister Crowley, said to have "been responsible for running a community in Northern Sicily where a number of children had been rumored to have disappeared in connection with Satanic masses." (https://espionagehistoryarchive. com/2016/03/05/occult-mi6-dennis-wheatley/)

An article by an ex-FBI agent states that the bureau "in recent years has focused on child sexual abuse and the alleged human sacrifice of missing children . . . Recently a flood of law enforcement seminars and conferences have dealt with satanic and ritualistic crime. These training conferences have various titles, such as 'Occult in Crime,' 'Satanic Cults,' 'Ritualistic Crime Semina,' 'Satanic Influences in Homicide'." (https://www.ojp.gov/pdffiles1/ Digitization/136592NCJRS.pdf)

So, child ritualistic killings, be them by witch doctors, cult leaders, satanic secret societies, or pedophile rings, are not myths, but very real. The African continent may have more than its share of child sacrifices than other continents. This is an evil driven by ignorance, superstitions, poverty, warped religious practices, and the greed bred by globalization and colonization.

Consequently, I think the horror genre should not be used to preserve this evil, even as it is needed as material to instill terror in the narrative. Rather, it should be used as a weapon to expose it for what it is: a vile practice that must be stopped by every means. I've been accused by some people of perpetuating negative stereotypes in my works. I believe those people are in denial, just as the West and other parts of the globe are in denial about a lot of their own societal evils. My writing is therefore a kind of naming and shaming, hoping that the powers might be shamed into doing something about this stain on their nations, and start making the necessary changes, starting with ending corruption and poverty, as well as reeducating their people. In fact, the Nigerian legislative house put forward a motion this year to end ritualistic killings. (https://www.cfr.org/blog/ritual-killings-nigeria-reflect-mounting-desperation-wealth-and-security-amid-creeping)

There are a few stories in which female jealousy is the key element of the horror unleashed. Polygamy seems also to be one of the triggers of violence. What is your position on these subjects? Do you women particularly prone to rivalry, and do you consider polygamy as a potentially violent social construction?
Different societies live by different cultures and belief systems. It is my personal belief that one dominant group should not impose their culture on others. This was the scourge of colonization in the modern era, and wars in the ancient eras, when the dominant nations wiped out the cultures of the subjugated, and replaced them with their own. Monogamy is a Western concept. Many other cultures, from Africa, Asia, and the Middle East, all practice some form of polygamy.

While I personally abhor the practice, due to my early indoctrinations and adult inclinations, I know many family friends who are happy in that environment. The children are united by their father's name and his bloodline. They don't view themselves as their mother's children, but rather, as their father's blood-heirs. The wives are united in a bond of sisterhood, forming a visible chain and shield that keeps their husband's children safe. They take pride in being the wives of the man and the mother of his children, especially if they have sons for their husbands. The American TV shows like *Sister Wives*, *My Five Wives*, and *Polygamy, USA* all depict women making conscious choices to enter into polygamous marriages, despite the freedoms and protections accorded them by Western laws. So, polygamy can be something that works perfectly in cultures where it is the norm, and the women have not been exposed to the Western monogamous system that breeds jealousy and rivalry.

However, it becomes a different story in cultures where choice is taken away from women and they are forced into marriages, be them polygamous or monogamous marriages. Then, polygamy becomes an evil problem that seeks to deprive women of their human rights and freedoms. I dare not speculate on whether women are more prone to rivalry than men, especially since all wars and assassinations in history have been mainly instigated by huge male egos and rivalries. But yes, polygamy can definitely trigger violence in cultures more used to monogamy, just as stepmothers are the greatest triggers of evil and violence in many horror narratives, alas.

The portrait you give of gender relations in Nigeria is often quite bleak and violent. Have you been criticized for this? If yes, how do you react to these critics? And do you feel that the horror genre gives you the opportunity to tackle gender questions that could be overseen?

Gender relations in Nigeria, just like many patriarchal nations worldwide, is quite bleak and violent. In fact, gender relations worldwide are bleak and violent, if one takes into account the statistics of violent crimes and domestic abuse perpetrated against women by men. Like Nigeria, many cultures have their own local practices and beliefs that continue to repress, abuse, and disempower the women in their various communities. I'm sure readers of works from other regions will encounter the same degree of violence against women as contained in my works. Let's recall Stephen King's *Rose Madder*, for instance. Thankfully, till date, this is one aspect of my work that I've yet to receive any criticisms, and I'm thankful I can continue to use the medium of horror to highlight this gender inequality to a broader audience.

CHAPTER NINETEEN

Cat Rambo

Cat Rambo (born in 1963) is an award-winning American science fiction and fantasy writer. Notable works: *Exiles of Tabat* (novel, 2021), *You Sexy Thing* (novel, 2021).

Dear Cat, thank you very much for accepting this interview. This book is going to focus specifically on the notions of "gender" and "genre," two very fluid notions much discussed today. In this light, can you tell us about your background and how this, in your eyes, influenced the person and the writer you are today?
I was one of the first students to receive a certificate from the Gender Studies program at the University of Notre Dame, which launched while I was a student there. The support and mentorship I got from the faculty there was instrumental in creating me as I am today. I've got a shout-out to one of them, Dr. Charlene Avallone, in one of my short stories, "All the Pretty Little Mermaids," which appeared in *Asimov's Science Fiction* magazine a number of years back and references a lot of feminist theory. (I'm aware of and relish the irony of such a story appearing in a magazine named for one of science fiction's most notorious gropers.) So, feminism has played a part in both my life and my writing for a long time.

That's just one facet of that feminism, of course. Games, books, plants, and particularly people, so many things have gone into my life, and I'm vividly grateful for that. I was lucky enough to have multiple examples of excellent women to follow: my grandmother was a YA fiction writer, my mother a journalist, and the inimitable Sarah Bird, a local woman who co-owned the Griffon Bookstore, and who I learned so much from about being unapologetically who I am.

Speculative fiction has traditionally been regarded as a male-oriented genre. Before the advent of second-wave feminism and the gay liberation movement in the 1960s, women writers were denied recognition not as much by publishing houses as by science fiction nominations and awards. Even today, science fiction is still considered as mainly appealing to men and fantasy as being more welcoming to women. How do you feel about this gender-oriented differentiation among genres?

There were definitely women writing (and editing!) then, but you're right that they got overlooked not just by awards but often by anthologies and "best of" collections. Science fiction has been one of the fields where the pressure put on women and writers of color meant that they had to be truly great to make it: Octavia E. Butler comes to mind, for one, as do Connie Willis and Ursula K. Le Guin. It's infuriating. It gets in the way of both writers and readers, and it's just foolish and unproductive.

Do you think women in horror and science fiction are in a better position today than when you began to write? Do you feel any gendered resistance in the milieu or in the reviews?

I do think they're in a better position, and that we've got a better understanding of things like the fluidity of gender, and the existence of nonbinary folks, or of how institutional gender-based discrimination operates, and so it's easier to recognize and point things out. The #MeToo movement has—at least, I hope—enabled a lot of people to speak out about abusers and predators in a way that I don't remember happening when I was coming of age. And there is a growing understanding that the wealthy ruling class uses some of this against us, setting groups against each other in an endless "my -ism beats yours" splintering that weakens solidarity.

But sure, there is still plenty of gendered resistance. Every time someone talks about "cancel culture," it's a resistance to that sort of change. The idea that horror and science fiction could and should do better in terms of inclusivity and representation gets painted as trendy or "virtue signaling." (What a weird idea, that being virtuous is shameful and should be hidden away.) I see people sneering at romance, traditionally the realm of women writers. I see women writers, writers of color, QUILTBAG writers all having to be superlative in order to make it into publishing, let alone survive there.

Did you encounter any discrimination specifically related to your gender in your writing career?
Of course, I have. Every woman has, I think, at least in some form of how I'd define discrimination. Minority writers, trans writers, disabled writers—everyone outside the norm gets clubbed by that norm on a regular basis. Some have the economic or psychic resources to ignore it, but it's something that we all should be acknowledging, not to mention actively battling.

This is one of the paradoxes of the internet. On the one hand, it connects us and lets us communicate the knowledge and support that we need in order to fight back, to name and normalize and other forms of resistance. But it charges a high price for that admission in the form of trolls and other online attacks and harassment. Women and minorities get more of that hostile attention, to the point where many of us get driven off the internet or forced to minimize exposure to it.

There is today an ongoing debate around the word "genre" in the science fiction/horror milieu. Some agree with Ursula K. Le Guin that it is socially prejudiced; others claim that it is an essential and necessary literary "identity." What is your position on the subject?
Genre is a marketing term used to help corporations finetune their advertising.

What is determinant in your choice of the genres you chose to write in?
I write the sort of stuff I want to read.

The 1960s and 70s are perhaps the most influential decades in the study of gender in speculative fiction. Not only was there an influx of female speculative fiction writers, but also many of these writers applied feminist theory to speculative fiction (Ursula K. Le Guin, Angela Carter, etc.). At the same time, the emergence of African-American female voices brought to light the intersectionality between gender and race. It is as if speculative fiction genres offered better than others the opportunity to challenge social conventions,

especially gender, and to explore alternative sexualities and alliances. Is it the case in your work? Have you been influenced by specific writers of this generation?

Absolutely. Joanna Russ, first and foremost. In fact, when I was applying to graduate writing programs, I applied to University of Washington, but wrote to Russ beforehand and basically said, "I am applying because YOU teach here, please let me know if you're about to go elsewhere." She kindly replied, and of course that was the only program I did not get accepted into.

Beyond the names you supply, there were Octavia E. Butler, Vonda N. McIntyre, James Tiptree, Jr., and of course, the prolific Andre A. Norton, whose YA work I devoured as a teen, those rich years when she was cranking them out in the 1970s. And a number of nongenre writers, including John Barth and Grace Paley. I read fast and I love to do it. I started reading in pre-internet days, when there were only three TV channels and I would do things like work through all of Trollope in a summer.

In your eyes, what renders speculative fiction apt to engage in sexual politics? Do you feel that it is easier for genre literature to accommodate contemporary post-identitarian claims than it is in mainstream culture?

People smarter than me have mentioned that speculative fiction is as much about the time in which it's being written as its putative settings, and that's true. I don't know that I'd make a distinction between speculative and mainstream so much as I'd draw a line between actual writing and commercially motivated fiction, because the latter is always going to be less prone to making people uncomfortable as a strategy.

In "genre fiction" such as fantasy, speculative fiction, and other relatively formulaic genres, characters are usually stereotyped. Yet the world into which they are set is often entirely idiosyncratic. How do you manage to negotiate this tension with respect to gender images?

I don't agree that they're "usually" stereotyped, but we may be working with different groups when we're thinking about this. I read a lot of contemporary speculative fiction and it seems to me there's fewer stereotypes in it than a lot of other manifestations of fiction.

The several subcategories that emerged with regard to speculative fiction (gay, lesbian, transgender, feminist, black, etc.), enhanced by the different anthologies that we can find in the market, not only signify the portrayal of specific identities or communities, but also each of them seems to address a specific audience. Do you write/ with a gendered audience in mind?
Nope.

Do you think that speculative fiction works are differently structured when addressed to traditionally under-portrayed individuals or communities? Is the portrayal of a minority specifically addressed to those that feel portrayed in these works?
I find these questions difficult to answer because to me they seem to presume a lot more deliberate consideration of the reader while writing than I do, particularly in first drafts. I am sure there are writers that think about that more than I do, but in my experience it's a consideration that gets in the way of word flow. These are things I think about in the rewrite and polish, perhaps, but even there I am thinking more about the story and its needs than the reader's. This is partially because I have found you cannot predict the reader.

In your novel and stories, your main characters are very often tough single, bi-sexual, lesbian, or even pansexual women. Do you feel that genre is more open to character identities than "established literature"?
Nope, there are plenty of them elsewhere in literature, too. In my opinion.

In your *Tabat Space* fantasy series, the world you describe is based on social and political violence, and yet is sexually very free and open, as it supposedly was under the Roman Empire. This actually goes against the general assumption that more sexual freedom equates to a more democratic society. Does this paradox illustrate your personal view on the ongoing gender issues?
It is primarily because I didn't want to perpetuate or bother adhering to a social structure that I find regressive and unpleasant. This is one reason to write fantasy, to write worlds different from our own.

In your latest novel at the time of this interview, *You Sexy Thing*, you take on the space-opera genre and describe intergalactic species erotica, as Philip Jose Farmer did in the 1970s. Is that a way, for you, to subvert a traditionally rather puritan genre? And is it linked with an underlying political motive?

Actually, I was just having fun with it. The book was written with myself in mind as the reader, someone who wanted a frothy space opera with a lot of banter, some adventure, and solid, interesting relationships between a varied group of people. I wrote it thinking about self-publishing it, and then my agent said: nuh uh, and sold it to Tor.

I love these characters, and I've got a ten-book arc sketched out for them, with book two turned in and book three bubbling away. They are hell of a fun to write. Any gender analysis, any political stuff that's seeping through, that's me, that's the stuff I think about and try to act in ethical accordance with on a daily basis. When I write though, I let it slide to the back burner and don't worry about it. I just write.

CHAPTER TWENTY

Tricia Reeks

Tricia Reeks (born in 1962) is an American publisher and the founder of Meerkat Press in 2015.

Dear Tricia Reeks, thank you very much for accepting to answer these few questions. This book is going to focus specifically on the notions of "gender" and "genre" and how they intersect in speculative fiction and horror. In this light, can you tell us about your background and how this, in your eyes, influenced the person and publisher you are today?
There have been several key influencers in my publishing persona. One is the fact that I am a woman, and I have always been interested in women's issues. Another is that my mother was a voracious reader of speculative fiction. So, I had access at an early age to a library that ranged from pulp science fiction to the supernatural and the occult. I developed a keen taste for these genres, and especially darker fiction. Over the course of my reading life, books such as Margaret Atwood's *The Handmaid's Tale*, Shirley Jackson's *We Have Always Lived in the Castle*, and Toni Morrison's *Beloved* are the type of books that hit my sweet spot of masterful writing about issues that made a big impact on me. And my reading taste greatly influences what I publish. More so than any other factor.

How do you feel about this gender-oriented differentiation among genres? Do you feel it still exists?
As a reader, I don't often notice that differentiation. I expect that if I was a writer, I would be better positioned to notice it.

Do you feel any gendered resistance in the publishing milieu or in the reviews of the books you publish?

In my short time in the publishing industry—our first publication was late 2015—and more specifically small press publishing, there has been a focus on correcting gender-based imbalances that exist. I see this regularly with small press genre publishers and with organizations such as SFWA (Science Fiction & Fantasy Writers Association). My hope is that this is sustained, and not just a "trend." Because as we see with the current state of gender equality in general, it will take effort and attention to keep a forward motion. From my standpoint, the bigger resistance I encounter is my small press books going up against the Big Five (or whatever that number may have decreased to at the time of this printing) in trying to get attention from reviewers and the media.

Did you encounter any discrimination specifically related to your gender in your publishing career?

I have been fortunate in that I've never encountered any recognizable discrimination related to my gender in publishing.

There is today an ongoing debate around the word "genre" in the science fiction/horror milieu. Some agree with Ursula K. Le Guin that it is socially prejudiced; others claim that it is an essential and necessary literary "identity." What is your position on the subject? What has determined your choice of literature as a publisher?

As I have a background in computer science, I understand that at the data level, there is a need for categorization of books. It is necessary in libraries, at retailers both online and bricks-and-mortar, and to help readers sift through the enormous volume of books available to read to find those they are most interested in. That said, I feel that there needs to be a more frequent analysis and update to the categories. As a publisher, I have the hardest time categorizing my books because I love genre-bending fiction. My favorite is literary-leaning dark speculative fiction. An example is a book we published by **Eugen Bacon**, titled *Claiming T-Mo*. It is literary to its core, based on the strength and beauty of the prose, the deep character development and themes of otherness, and gender and race oppression, yet it is a fantasy novel with an immortal priest, and a Jekyll-and-Hyde-type character. But it is also science fiction, including interplanetary characters and travel. Similarly,

J. S. Breukelaar's *The Bridge*, defies clean categorization. It is beautifully written with complex feminist themes. There are witches and magic that are pure fantasy, hybrid humans that are pure science fiction, and a dead sister that just won't go away—pure horror. Not easy to fit those into the current Bisac structure[1] in a way that is meaningful to someone searching for that kind of book.

The 1960s and 70s are perhaps the most influential decades in the study of gender in speculative fiction and horror. Not only was there an influx of female writers, but also many of these writers applied feminist theory to speculative fiction (Ursula K. Le Guin, Angela Carter, Shirley Jackson, etc.). At the same time, the emergence of African-American female voices brought to light the intersectionality between gender and race. It is as if speculative fiction and the horror genres offered better than others the opportunity to challenge social conventions, especially gender, and to explore alternative sexualities and alliances. What, in your eyes, renders speculative fiction and horror genres apt to engage in sexual politics?
Speculative fiction is the perfect genre for exploring social issues, including sexual politics. We go into it understanding that we must suspend belief. What we might subconsciously refuse to see in our actual society can somehow be more palatable when presented as a different species, or on a different planet (we'd never do that here, right?). In my early twenties when I read *The Handmaid's Tale*, it hit me hard, thinking about being a female in a world like that, yet here in the US, we find ourselves in *The Handmaid's Tale: The Prequel*.

Meerkat Press covers a variety of genres, from horror to speculative fiction and fantasy. Your authors also offer a varied background, both gender-wise and culturally. Do you consciously try to mirror the diversity of identities in your publishing and in the choice of your authors, or do you see it just as a reflection of the evolution of the times?
I think that it is a bit of both of these factors. From the standpoint of it being a reflection of our times, modern technology allows me

---

[1]The BISAC Subject Headings List (https://bisg.org/page/BISACSubjectCodes).

to discover authors from anywhere in the world and provides exposure to fiction that is culturally diverse. And since we are open to unagented submissions, there is no gatekeeper limiting who or what gets in. At that point, it is up to me. Most of what we publish is based on my reading taste, but fortunately, I have diverse tastes in style, genre, and story. In deciding sometimes between multiple works that are equal in quality, I have made decisions based on diversity. I have also made some choices on subgenres that are not necessarily going to make it to my personal To Be Read pile, but that I wanted to include for variety and thus when I came across what I felt to be really good work in that genre, I pursued it.

Speculative fiction and horror have often represented situations of sexual, family, or political oppression, and many of the books you have published focus on these themes. As a publisher, are you specifically looking for these themes? Do you think genre literature has a specific identity that allows it to tackle these themes for a larger audience than mainstream literature?
As a person who has always rooted for the underdog and who loves darker books that leave me somewhat unsettled, it seems to work out that way. Oppression in any of its forms lends itself to that kind of book. Speculative fiction and horror are perfect for these kinds of themes as they provide an open canvas for portraying harsh themes in a way that can be less threatening because it is fantasy.

I have noticed that you have about a 50:50 ratio of male and female writers. Is that voluntary?
It isn't a scientific approach by any means, but I do try to ensure that I include a variety of genders and genres.

You publish both male and female writers. Do you feel there is a difference in writing between the genders? Are you sensitive to their narrative angles?
I do have an internal bias as there are times I specifically think I want to read a certain kind of book and I subconsciously think I should be looking for a specific gender of an author. For example, if I'm looking to feel the way I felt after reading Toni Morrison, I might find myself looking for a female author. But if I'm looking to feel the way I felt after reading Brian Evenson, I might find myself looking for a male author. It is too easy to equate a style to a gender

and that is such a broad generalization. I recently read Susanna Clarke's *Pirinesi* and if I'd had to guess without knowing first, I would have thought it was written by a man. So, I know that my internal bias is very limiting.

Do you hope to make a difference with Meerkat Press when it comes to gender issues and narratives (whether cis or LGBT+)? If yes, in what way?
I think that my greatest hope is to share fiction with the world that makes me feel something that I want others to feel, too. Since the things that make me feel the most tend to be social issues, then I think it will be a natural outcome.

CHAPTER TWENTY-ONE

Priya Sharma

Priya Sharma (born in 1971) is an award-winning English-born novelist and short-stories writer. Notable works: *All The Fabulous Beasts* (short-story collection, 2018), *Ormeshadow* (novella, 2019), *Pomegranates* (novella, 2022).

Dear Priya Sharma, thank you very much for accepting to be part of this volume, which will focus specifically on the notions of "gender" and "genre." Can you tell us about your background and how these notions had an influence on the person and the writer you are today?
My parents emigrated from India to the UK in 1968 and I grew up in a market town in the northwest of England. We stuck out like a sore thumb as one of only two Asian families. I felt both inside and outside of everything. It made me see the world in a different way to my peers. It made me compartmentalize bits of my life, too, which I do to some extent now. I think it also colored my decision to pursue medicine rather than literature or creative writing at university. With the long lens of the retrospectoscope I think that was driven by several things—to help people, a love of science, the need to be financially independent, wanting to belong and be respected, but also to be privy to people's most vulnerable moments. Being a doctor is very privileged in that respect. I came to writing later in life as a result, but having a particular set of experiences to bring to it.

I grew up with a love of Greek and Hindu myths, my brother's DC and Marvel comics, Roald Dahl's children's books, and Thomas

Hardy. TV-wise, there was *Tales of the Unexpected*, the BBC's *Armchair Thriller* and *Sapphire and Steel*, the Richard Chamberlain versions of *The Man in the Iron Mask* and *The Count of Monte Cristo*. As a teen I discovered Stephen King, Clive Barker, Angela Carter, and *Twin Peaks*.

Did you encounter any discrimination specifically related to your gender in your writing career?
Not directly or openly. My experience has been very positive, but I know that's not the case for other writers. Discrimination can be a very slippery thing. It's not always overt or easy to call out.

The part of me that is haunted by Imposter Syndrome worries that other writers think I've benefited from positive discrimination with regard to my gender and ethnicity, rather than any success I've had—based on merit.

I'm not sure if anyone's done a robust statistical analysis of markets which reveal bias or discrimination within genre writing. I've heard editors say that they want to see more diversity in the writers submitting to them, so I wonder where the disconnection is. I don't know what the submission rates are in regards to gender, but it would be interesting to break that down. Is it that there are less women submitting, and if yes, why?

Audiences are more sophisticated than people give them credit for. They'll seek out the work they want. I hope publishers are responding to that, if only for financial reasons.

What do you think of the position of women in horror and fantasy today? Do you feel any gendered resistance in the milieu or in the reviews?
I've been going to two UK annual meetings for a few years—British Fantasy Con and the now sadly no-more Edgelit. Both conferences are writer- rather than fan-based. I've made great friends there and feel part of a supportive community. Sadly, that's not everyone's experience though.

That's not to say it doesn't exist. The controversy over the Hugo Awards is well documented. Certain groups felt that the ballot was becoming too diverse and orchestrated a block vote.

There is today an ongoing debate around the word "genre" in the science fiction/horror milieu. Some agree with Ursula K. Le Guin

that it is socially prejudiced; others claim that it is an essential and necessary literary "identity." What is your position on the subject?
It's definitely a ghettoized branch of fiction. All you need to do is look at the Sunday supplements on books and the shelf-space in bookshops. I went into a wonderful bookshop in Bath, where they file all adult fiction together, regardless of genre, and I enjoyed seeing that. Not because I feel embarrassed of the genre label, but because I hope it led to sales of genre novels to readers who might not have picked up those books otherwise.

It's great to see horror films shortlisted for Oscars and BAFTAs, but I'm not convinced that will filter into bookshops in the same way. Repackage a book as gothic or as a ghost story and it becomes more commercial. There's work that is now billed as crime that has horror/supernatural elements that could put it in both markets.

It is double-edged in that what it's fostered are lots of indie presses publishing exciting work (such as Dead Ink, Unsung Stories, Undertow Publications, PS Publishing). There's also a hugely active and supportive community of horror writers, editors, and publishers. We're not drinking magnums of champagne on our royalties, but we have an absolute blast.

The genre label evokes preconceived ideas in the wider public's minds but I embrace it. I think it's about education and marketing. People who tell me they have no interest in fantasy praise *Game of Thrones*. Those who don't like speculative fiction love *Arrival*. As to horror, look at the love for Susan Hill's *The Woman in Black*.

I think it's a label I now wear as a badge of honor. It evokes prejudice from people who actually know very little about the quality and breadth of work available under the genre banner.

You write horror and dark fantasy. What is determinant in your choice of these genres?

I'm best known for my short-story collection, *All the Fabulous Beasts*, which is only about half of my published short stories. Undertow Publications' editor, Michael Kelly, has a very particular vision for his press: dark, weird fiction. He carefully curated which stories he wanted from my back catalog. It resulted in a tightly themed collection with a dark tone. The lighter fantasy stories are uncollected to date.

I'm writing more and more for anthologies that are horror/dark fantasy as a result, as that's what I'm associated with. There's a lot of latitude though, depending on the editor. Horror is broad. It can be a shadow or a sledgehammer.

I love it when the characters are strong enough to dictate where their story ends up. I once wrote a story for a sea-based horror anthology that ended up as a dark coming-of-age story. It got rejected on the grounds of it being strange but not horror. I didn't regret my choices. Horror should serve the story, not the other way around.

What writers have you been influenced by? Was their gender important to you?
I was encouraged to read anything I wanted without censorship when I was growing up. I've never consciously chosen books based on the author's gender. I loved works by Angela Carter, Jeanette Winterson, Clive Barker, Sarah Waters, Jim Crace, Alice Walker, Toni Morrison, Isabella Allende, Iain Banks, Cormac McCarthy, Sarah Hall, Michael Cunningham, and Neil Gaiman. Oh, and **Ellen Datlow** and Terri Windling's series of fairy tales, the stories of my childhood suddenly all grown-up.

I was always interested in content and style over the author's gender. I loved Jeanette Winterson's magical realism, her playfulness with time and structure. That she was a writer about sexuality in a way I'd not seen before was an education for me. I am a huge fan of Sarah Waters and her stories are thrilling.

The only thing I find hard to forgive in a book is dullness, and dullness isn't gender-specific.

In your opinion, what renders horror genres apt to engage in sexual politics?
I think horror, speculative fiction, and fantasy are perfect vehicles for politics. They are metaphor. They are extrapolation. Each decade of genre writing reflects the concerns and fears of that period, and questions social conventions.

Horror is about life at the edge of our comfort zones, where we're afraid, powerless, and have lost control. The monstrous represents our baser selves, including carnality, so it's an easy way of exploring sex and sexual politics. Sex has been entwined with horror from its beginning. The gothic burns with it. *Carmilla* by Sheridan Le Fanu, Bram Stoker's *Dracula*, *The Monk* by Matthew Lewis.

In film we have gems like *Cat People* and *Ginger Snaps* that explore female sexuality. Sadly, horror is associated with torture porn and sexual violence, but there's been a reinvention of the Final Girl trope. One of my favorites is "Final Girl Theory," a short story by A. C. Wise that is included in her collection *The Ghost Sequences*. Another is *Alien*, which I'd argue is a horror film set in space. Ripley is the ultimate Final Girl.

As a marginalized genre, the indie horror press has much more freedom in what they publish and can foster new voices and writers. "The Beauty" by Aliyah Whiteley (*Unsung Stories*) is sexual politics via body horror. In a post-woman society, a fungi-based life form springs from the graves of dead women. It's frightening and disturbing, also touching, asking questions about gender roles.

Do you think genres have adapted to the new post-identitarian gender claims, such as expressed by the LGBT+ movement?
Not yet. It's something that is still evolving. It's not just an issue in genre fiction, but a more general one. It's currently being played out on social media and causing a lot of hurt and polarization.

The several subcategories that emerged with regard to horror and fantasy (gay, lesbian, transgender, feminist, black, etc.), enhanced by the different anthologies that we can find in the market, not only signify the portrayal of specific identities or communities, but also each of them seems to address a specific audience. Do you write with a gendered audience in mind?
No, I write for myself without thinking about who is going to read it. This is when I get to explore themes and ideas for myself. I enjoy writing the most when I'm at my least self-conscious. I think writing with a specific audience in mind is folly. You won't please everyone and you dilute your vision.

Your first collection of short stories, *All the Fabulous Beasts*, has animality (in the largest sense of the term) as its central theme. Do you feel that this topic is or can be gender-related?
I've used this as a way to channel ideas around sex, sexuality, birth, and parenting. Animal nature sometimes diverges from the well-delineated gender lines we imagine. For example, male seahorses have a brood pouch where the females deposit their eggs for

fertilization. They gestate there until the male gives birth to them. I find that fascinating.

Animality doesn't have to be synonymous with brutality, the sensual needn't be crude or coarse. That aspect of our nature is deeper than gender roles. There's a beast in all of us regardless of gender identity. That's what I find interesting. What is it about life that makes us call on that beast? I like the sense of the beast within us as something more honest and instinctive, capable of great trust, nobility, and tenderness as well as brutality.

Women are very often in the center of these stories, although not always the main character. In your novella *Ormeshadow*, for instance, the main character is a young boy. How do you feel about writing through the prism of another gender?
I've written quite a few short stories with male protagonists, which are uncollected. I'd hate to be restricted to writing through the single prism of my own experiences. Sometimes you need to step outside that to tell the story you want to tell—it demands a different point of view. With *Ormeshadow*, I didn't feel confident about writing a child in first person, so I moved to third person. If you're going to inhabit another skin, then you need to know you can fit into it.

In *All the Fabulous Beasts* and *Ormeshadow*, animals and monsters are more than often linked to a form of power, albeit a cursed one, running in a family. Would you consider this trope as a specific feminine theme of womanhood and motherhood?
The Bloody Chamber by Angela Carter had a huge influence on me. I loved the fact it addressed the animal nature of women as equal to men's. It was sensuous, feminine, and powerful. I think those animal themes speak to the otherness inside ourselves and are perfect for genre fiction.

The monstrous as a trope isn't gender-specific in my opinion, but I felt it was apt for the issues I wanted to write about. Women's bodies go through such dramatic changes physiologically: menarche, motherhood, and menopause. I have severe endometriosis and fibroids which blighted my twenties and thirties. Over the ten years it took me to write these stories, I was thinking a lot about definitions of womanhood, parenthood, and the effects of illness.

My writing seems to return again and again to secrets and power dynamics within families. Monstrosity seemed to fit well within that frame.

Would you consider yourself a "woman writer," a "genre writer," or just a "writer"?
I still struggle to call myself a writer, if I'm being completely honest. I'm not sure when I'll feel I've earned the word, so I'm grateful and proud to be called any of those.

CHAPTER TWENTY-TWO

Angela Slatter

Angela Slatter (born in 1968) is an award-winning Australian folk-horror, urban fantasy, and fantasy writer. Notable works: *Sourdough and Other Stories* (collection, 2010), *All the Murmuring Bones* (novel, 2022).

Dear Angela Slatter, thank you very much for accepting to be part of this volume, focused on the topics of genre and gender. In this light, can you tell us about your background and how this, in your eyes, influenced the person and the writer you are today?
I've always been a big reader and read everything as a young reader—including a whole lot of things that I was probably too young for. Classics, thrillers, literary novels, fairy tales, horror, crime. Anything and everything. And my dad was a homicide detective, so I had a possibly unhealthy interest in crime, and heard a lot of interesting stories over the dinner table. I was left unsupervised and uncensored as a reader—possibly something my parents regret now!—and so I read everything and anything from the classics to the pulpiest of pulps, from Shakespeare to Phantom comics. So, fairy tales from my mother and crime stories from my dad have pretty much influenced the reading I sought for myself as a writer and also the stories I write today.

Do you think women in horror and fantasy are in a better position today than when you began to write? Do you feel any gendered resistance in the milieu or in the reviews?
I'd like to think so, and mostly we don't have to take on male pseudonyms now in order to get published. But there are still a lot

of anthologies with very few women in the table of contents. Whenever someone brings it up, you hear the defense that the editor didn't know where to find women in horror—because we're naturally camouflaged, apparently—or that women don't write horror, or that women don't submit to horror markets. If you can't find us, it's probably because you're not looking. There are also a lot of women writing some of the best crime today—and I always say that crime is the sibling of horror.

Did you encounter any discrimination specifically related to your gender in your writing career?
Nothing overt. I was fortunate to be invited to submit to high-profile markets based on work published elsewhere. But among reviewers there's still the occasional complaint along the lines of "not all men" due to the fact that there are males in my stories who are not very nice. There are also women in my stories who aren't very nice either, but no one seems to whine about that. Statistically women are more likely to be the victims of violent crime perpetrated by men, often men who are their partners or relatives and who should, in theory, be protecting them. But it seems we're often just more easily accessible victims of temper tantrums and misdirected rage. So, reviews that are essentially "You're a mean lady" are not especially useful.

You write horror, dark fantasy, and "horror-noir." What is determinant in your choice of these genres?
If it's a story being written specifically in response to an invitation, it will often depend on the theme of the anthology, if the market is more skewed toward horror or fantasy or fairy tale. If it's something I'm writing for one of the Sourdough world mosaics, it will likely be more a dark fairy tale than anything. If it's just a story I'm writing for no reason it will probably be more "proper" or traditional horror in a modern setting—generally about the ill we do to each other, often those we're closest to.

The novel I'm editing at the moment, *The Path of Thorns*, is a gothic tale, sort of *Jane Eyre* meets *Frankenstein*, because I wanted to write something that was a conversation with Mary Shelley's great work. There's a lot of horror, a lot of monstrous behavior from everyone involved. *All the Murmuring Bones*, the novel before this, was again a gothic fantasy with a heroine who takes a very pragmatic view of what she needs to do to survive—she never worries about being "polite" or whether anyone will like her or not.

There is today an ongoing debate around the word "genre" in the science fiction/horror milieu. Some agree with Ursula K. Le Guin that it is socially prejudiced; others claim that it is an essential and necessary literary "identity." What is your position on the subject?
Aaaah, I think it's a marketing term that's gotten out of control. You can ask "What's the genre?" out of pure curiosity. Or you can say "Genre?" with a sneer and change the meaning immediately. It's become something that can be an insult—fewer things sound more cutting than a literary critic letting the words "genre novel" drip from their pen. It should simply be a guide for readers, not a marker of supposed quality. Margaret Atwood is regarded as a literary writer, but her books are speculative in nature—she starts from a point of something that's already existing in the world and then asks "What if?" *The Handmaid's Tale, Oryx and Crake*—all do exactly what science fiction does: speculate. All fiction posits, really, about possibilities if not probabilities. The idea is to make a reader think, even if they're not aware you're gently cracking open their brain.

You'll get readers who say: "Oh, no. I have never read science fiction!" But you will find Atwood on their shelves. In a way, I think the term "genre" has started to obscure what books are actually about. Le Guin might well be right.

What writers have you been influenced by? Was their gender important to you?
Ah, when I was younger, I read a lot of Stephen King, Clive Barker, Richard Laymon, Shaun Hutson, Phil Rickman, James Herbert— because they were the horror writers who were published. It took a long while for me to find Mary Shelley, but I read the Brontës early on and realized they had a good deal of horror in their works. In my teens I discovered Tanith Lee, Nancy Kress, Sheri S. Tepper, and Jane Gaskell—I return to their books frequently—and they're all writers who mix dark fantasy with horror in varying degrees. I'd say the two short horror stories that stick in my mind from my early teens are "The Chosen Vessel" by Barbara Baynton and "The Tower" by Marghanita Laski—they've never left me and I hope I manage to channel in my work something of the raw terror I felt the first time I read them.

It was important to find female writers in my chosen genres because I didn't want to write like a man. Oftentimes, we're so influenced by male writers because for a long while that was all you had to read—you didn't realize there were female writers out there, because they often weren't getting the same degree of exposure. I teach creative writing and more than once I've gone back to female students and said: 'You're writing like a man—there's a lot of ingrained misogyny in this story, your female characters are acting like male characters, thinking like male characters. Is this intentional? Or are you just mimicking what you've read?" Nine times out of ten they'll come back and say they had no idea—they'd just read books by men in their chosen genre all the time, and that was what they'd patterned on. When they'd come back with new drafts, they'd actively changed the way they were writing these characters—and they were so much better, more authentic. I think we always need to be questioning our assumptions and ingrained habits as writers.

Women generally write such good male characters because they're good observers. Male writers frequently miss the target with female characters because they don't pay attention to what we say or do, they don't care how we think or what we want. They only care if we're pretty and our voice is soft and gentle . . .

What renders horror genres apt to engage in sexual politics?
Well, female bodies are the site of political discussions we're often not allowed to enter into. Abortion legislation. Reproductive regulation. We bleed once a month—it's the thing that makes us able to have children—yet menstruation is treated with disgust. We're unclean. In the US, rapists have rights over the bodies of their victims, if they get pregnant—thus continuing to perpetuate the rape and the victimization. We are wanted—men are so pissed off; if we refuse to sleep with them, some of them are "driven beyond reason"—but we are also despised. When someone hates themself for wanting something so much, that can translate into violence against the object of desire—without the object of desire having to do anything.

The latest example is Afghanistan—how quickly a bunch of angry men have wiped out women's rights almost overnight. How women are having to hide who they are, what they've achieved, burning their diplomas so no one might think their hearts and minds are the sites of possible rebellions. All these women had to disappear beneath a veil to hide what we are, so no one might know they're individuals. And that is freaking terrifying.

Our bodies are a site of horror that is imposed on us—our bodies are warzones. Our independence is taken from us. We have any degree of self-choice only at the sufferance of others. We had to fight for the right to vote. To work. For fair pay. For the right to own property. To get divorced. For the right to marry if we're gay—for any rights at all if we're trans. We're constantly having to fight. We're really fucking tired.

Do you write with the current debates around gender in mind? Are your characters influenced in any way by these discussions?
I write for myself. I write about the tides in my own life, and the experiences of women around me. Horror genres are women's lives. Women's lives are horror stories. If that comes through in my stories, it's no coincidence. But I also tend to write a lot of my stuff set in a world that's "not quite ours," so there's a degree of distancing there, I think.

Do you write with a gendered audience in mind?
Not especially. I think horror is more than just slashers going after girls. I think women are particularly well placed to write horror given the nature of our lives and how we exist in the world.

Your writing universe is essentially feminine. In your collections such as *Sourdough and Other Stories* and *The Bitterwood Bible and Other Recountings*, the narrative point of view is always centered around women protagonists, which is also true in your novels. Is this a reaction to male-dominated narratives in horror and fantasy, or does it come from another perspective?
These are the stories I want to tell. They're the stories I'm interested in—the tales women tell amongst themselves. The tales we tell to survive, to encode our experiences. I don't know if it's a reaction to male narratives—but a male narrative doesn't really reflect my experience. Why would I want or need to tell male narratives? There are enough of those around, told by men—why do women need to lend their voices to telling more male stories? Why do we have to keep supporting the dominant narrative?

Maria Dahvana Headley's *The Mere-Wife* makes the observation that—and I'm paraphrasing badly here—that women and gossip maintain the secrets of the world. Like there's this whispered knowledge that runs beneath the skin of the world, something denigrated by men, but it actually carries truth and wisdom and advice. In a lot of ways, I feel that that's also the essence of the fairy tale—that's why those tales are told and retold, remade and adapted. Created afresh for new generations, new tellers who say: "Listen, here is the thing you need to know."

Many of your short stories and all your novels deal with the mother–daughter relationship. Is this an intentional trope, and if so, why have you chosen to make it a recurrent echo in your fiction?
The mother–daughter relationship is one I always return to because it's fraught. The position of women has changed so much in the last hundred years or so. From suffragettes chaining themselves to the railings outside the Houses of Parliament in London, to the bra burnings of the 1970s, to the ongoing fight for equal pay, fighting against sexual harassment in the workplace (and everywhere else), the world that my grandmother and her sisters, my mother and her sisters, myself and my sister, my nieces all grew up in has changed so much.

Our mothers have taught us how to be in the world: whether to make ourselves small and quiet, or to make noise and claim our space—and often put ourselves in harm's way by doing the latter. I know my own mother wishes I were quieter. She's worried I'll offend, draw attention, that I'll seem unlikeable. But I don't think the advances and sacrifices of all these years, all these women who stood up and shouted until things changed, were so I could be a well-behaved, quiet, likable girl. If I'm not liked because I'm a woman with an opinion, then that's not about me. That's about a societal desire for women to be obedient and uncomplaining. And, quite frankly, fuck that.

Mothers teach their daughters how to move through the world. They teach their daughters how much to put up with; and they also (whether they realize it or not) teach their sons how much those sons can get away with. One of the themes I try to work with in my writing is that your daughter is going to be different to you and you should be okay with that. Whatever hopes you had for your child? They were *your* hopes, not your kid's—they're not you, not a chance for you to "do-over" life. They will have their own chances and hopes and dreams—you'll be afraid for them, but don't teach them to fear. Don't make them afraid to go outside, to draw attention.

I guess I'm hoping to teach others to make noise.

Verity Fassbinder, the heroine of your eponymous horror-noir trilogy (*Vigil, Corpselight,* and *Restoration*) has a very interesting name, with its androgynous and queer connotations. Is it a gender statement, a cultural reference, and homage to the German film director, all of this or something else altogether?

Nothing clever like that, I'm afraid! I chose Verity because it meant "truth" and I felt she was a seeker of truth, an uncoverer of lies and secrets. And I chose Fassbinder because I like the sound of it—and I wanted someone with a German name so I could reasonably have one of my first monsters (her father) as a *kinderfresser*, a child-eater.

Like Angela Carter you use fairy tales, mythology, and folklore in your fiction, and your feminine heroines often have to struggle in a male-dominated society and narratives. Do you feel like you're continuing Carter's feminist legacy in the subversion of these genres?

That would be nice! Carter is the best compliment, really. The funny thing is that I didn't read her until I did my MA in 2006—way back in my teens, I heard a radio program about *The Bloody Chamber*, but couldn't ever get a hold of it because it was in the days before the internet and ordering it (and the cost) was simply beyond reach. But, when I started doing my MA and was reading for that, there the book was on a library shelf . . . I guess it just had to be the right time.

Carter was so bold in her writing, and her life was basically that of someone breaking out and breaking away from a very sheltered and constricting upbringing. She was always breaking away, reinventing. I don't think you need to have had the same upbringing to want something new and fresh. Comfortable lives are great, but they often become stagnant without challenge—as does the brain—so I hope that I always continue to seek challenges. That my grasp always exceeds my reach.

CHAPTER TWENTY-THREE

Ann VanderMeer

Ann VanderMeer (born in 1957) is an award-winning American publisher and editor. Notable publications: *Sisters of The Revolution: A Feminist Speculative Fiction Anthology* (anthology, 2015), *The Big Book of Science Fiction* (anthology, 2016).

Thank you very much for accepting to answer these few questions. This book is going to focus specifically on the notions of "gender" and "genre" as we believe that both are equally intersectional and are either confronted by or confronting territorial positions of dominance. In this light, can you tell us about your background and how this, in your eyes, influenced the person and editor you are today?
My background is unusual for an editor. I came to this work purely out of my love for reading this type of fiction and also as a way to connect with my father. My educational background is in criminology (you would be surprised how often this comes in handy!) and my work experience is in the computer science field (I was a software developer for over thirty years).

My parents went through a horrible divorce when I was quite young. Because of this, my relationship with my father was constrained and difficult. I knew that he loved reading science fiction and at one time he even wanted to be a writer. He left behind the L. Frank Baum *Oz* books (all in perfect condition), which he had read as a child. I gravitated to them as soon as I could read. These books were not like anything else and even now I look at them in wonder. This was my introduction to fantastical fiction.

When I won the Hugo Award in 2009, my father was the first person I called. We both cried on the phone together. I told him the award was really more his than mine. And later for his eightieth birthday, he was my guest at WORLDCON (the World Science Fiction Convention) when it was in San Antonio (where he lived). We knocked heads a lot of the time, but he firmly believed that all of his daughters (there were five of us altogether!) could do anything we set our minds to do. I don't think it's a coincidence that we all enjoy this genre, whether books, movies, etc. It never crossed our minds that we couldn't do something we loved.

I started a magazine with a colleague who worked with me in the software company back in the late 1980s. No one told us we couldn't, and we didn't know what we didn't know, so we just dove in and made a million mistakes, but we loved it and we learned a lot. Later my partner left the publishing industry so I decided to continue the magazine on my own and expanded to books.

I have been blessed to be able to continue this work both at *Tor. com* with new fiction and with our huge mega-anthologies with reprinted works. In addition, I've been able to pursue my passion for translated fiction in most of the projects I've done. And now that Jeff and I are no longer working on any mega-anthologies, I am eager to spend more time working with and promoting the next generation of editors and anthologists. It's time to make space for them now.

Speculative fiction—and science fiction, in particular—has traditionally been regarded as a male-oriented genre. Before the advent of second-wave feminism and the gay liberation movement in the 1960s, women writers were denied recognition not as much by publishing houses as by science fiction nominations and awards. Some women, such as Alice Bradley Sheldon, even used male pseudonyms in order to get published. How do you feel about this gender-oriented differentiation among genres?
It's a shame that there were so many restrictions and roadblocks in the past, and not just in this field but in so many others. I saw this as well in the software industry. Back when I started working in software design (early 1980s), I would attend these national meetings with 200+ other software professionals. I was one of maybe three women in the country at that time. We stuck together, but were pleasantly surprised to find that most of the men welcomed

us as equals. However, as our numbers grew and we were no longer just a handful in a large group, the welcoming attitude shifted.

I recently was looking through some of my mother's old college yearbooks. She attended graduate school in business administration (with a focus on marketing) at the University of Miami in the 1950s. She was one of six women out of over three hundred in the entire class. Later she switched her major to get her MSW (Masters in Social Work) because the college guidance counselor told her that she wouldn't be able to get a job otherwise. She became a social worker but I don't think this was her passion.

I was taken aback about the lives of so many of these female writers while I was working on various anthology projects and researching their backgrounds. Often, I would see a bibliography of brilliant work and then a long stretch of nothing. I asked myself—why did these women stop writing? Did they start families? Did their husbands/lovers/families not provide the support they needed to continue writing? What brilliant pieces of fiction did we lose when these women stopped writing (or at least stop publishing)? Frustrating and sad.

It's the same with writers from marginalized communities, too. We could be missing some truly brilliant work because of prejudices and lack of support overall. *All* of these voices are important to the significance and the relevance of the genre. Why would anyone not want to explore everything possible? What are we afraid of? Isn't science fiction the literature of "what could be"?

Do you think women in horror and science fiction are in a better position today than when you began to work in publishing, in the late 1980s? Do you feel any gendered resistance in the milieu or in the reviews?
I do believe we're in a better position today, for a lot of reasons. One of them being that we now have many more "gatekeepers." It used to be that we had just a few editors/publishers in the field and if your writing wasn't to their taste, too bad. But now the field has opened up quite a bit and there are many more gatekeepers and places to get published. It's not enough to have more diversity in the writers and the fiction but we also need it in all aspects of the publishing world. Editors, art directors, sales and marketing, etc. You need all of these voices in the room.

That being said, I do believe that the more other writers see themselves reflected in what's being published, the more they see the possibilities for themselves moving forward. When I first took over the editor position for *Weird Tales* magazine, I reached out to as many women writers as I could. I was surprised by how few thought their work was good enough. It really was like pulling teeth to get them to send me a story. And then if I did get a story that didn't quite fit, I would urge them to send more but in far too many cases, it would be a long time, if ever, before I heard from them again.

Let's fast forward to an anthology I edited recently (2019) for the XPRIZE foundation titled *Current Futures*. I was tasked with finding women's voices, preferably from all over the world. I had a long list of amazing writers to contact. Almost everyone I queried said yes and wrote a fabulous story for the project!

I often think about my time teaching at the Clarion workshops. So many of the women writers would ask me how to balance their writing lives with their family lives. I never once got that question from a man. Although I am optimistic to see many more women in the field, this issue is still a challenge faced by many.

Did you encounter any discrimination specifically related to your gender in your editing career?
Absolutely! And surprisingly not just from men, but from other women, which still shocks me when I encounter it. I am still amazed at the number of professionals who won't respond to an email from me but will immediately jump through hoops to respond to my husband. And it doesn't matter how many times Jeff tells them they need to talk to me. Too often, people give credit to Jeff for my work. It's frustrating and he is constantly telling people to stop it, but it's difficult for them to understand that my work has value separately from Jeff. I am lucky to have a partner in Jeff because he frequently gives me credit and kudos for my work. He does this publicly as well. I'm not looking for accolades. I'm an editor because I prefer to be in the background and promote the creatives that I work with, but it is disheartening to see people publicly praise my work as someone else's.

Back when I was the editor for *Weird Tales*, I can't tell you the number of people, both men and women, who were sure that Jeff was the editor, not me. It was very frustrating because I worked very hard during my years at *Weird Tales*. And no, he didn't help me. I did that on my own. And yet, still today, he will get queries from people asking about *Weird Tales*. Sigh . . .

There is today an ongoing debate around the word "genre" in the science fiction/horror milieu. Some agree with Ursula K. Le Guin that it is socially prejudiced; others claim that it is an essential and necessary literary "identity." What is your position on the subject?
I have always had an issue with labels, especially when they are assigned to a writer. I can see the value of labels as a marketing term, but when you put a label on a writer, they can become locked in this box. It's limiting, and not just to the writer, but to the readers as well.

Instead of saying a story is science fiction or fantasy, how about if we looked at it more based on the themes? What if the *Game of Thrones* books were seen as epic geopolitical dramas covering decades and multiple powerful families? What if we considered *Lisey's Story* by Stephen King to be a novel about a marriage instead of only another horror novel? Many books can fit into multiple genres so the labels can be misleading.

This is one of the reasons I prefer a mix of writers and approaches in my projects. When Jeff and I launched *Best American Fantasy* in 2007, that was one of the goals—to show how you can bridge the gap between "mainstream" and "genre." (This was something I was doing back in the late 1980s, early 90s, with *The Silver Web*.) Our first volume included stories taken from the pages of literary magazines like the *Oxford American* and the *Georgia Review* as well as genre magazines like *Analog* and *Strange Horizons*. The challenge we faced with the series was where to place the books in the bookstores. In some instances, we even had chain bookstore buyers telling us to change the book covers to make them look more like genre books! The series was well-received, well-regarded but the booksellers weren't sure what to do with them. Alas, I think it was an idea before it's time, although I am happily seeing more of this genre-mixing now.

The 1960s and 70s are perhaps the most influential decades in the study of gender in speculative fiction and horror. Not only was there an influx of female writers, but also many of these writers applied feminist theory to speculative fiction (Ursula K. Le Guin, Angela Carter, Shirley Jackson, etc.). At the same time, the emergence of African-American female voices brought to light the intersectionality between gender and race. It is as if speculative fiction and the horror genres offered better than others the opportunity to challenge social

conventions, especially gender, and to explore alternative sexualities and alliances. What, in your eyes, renders speculative fiction and horror genres apt to engage in sexual politics?
Science fiction is the literature of "what could be" so it's a natural fit for exploring possible futures and playing around with history. As writers grapple with benign discontent, exploring gender politics (and honestly, any kind of politics) is especially ripe with possibilities.

I have seen in both speculative fiction and horror a tendency to be conservative and promote the status quo via these works of fiction. You can see that in many of the older stories written by those who have had more privilege. Not a blanket statement as there have been many genre-bending works over the years as well. And those are the stories that are still relevant today.

However, each individual writer has a lot of power when they sit down to create their worlds and place their characters within them. One of the most fascinating novels I've read recently was *Popisho* by Leone Ross. It's a mystery wrapped in a political and economic revolution as well as a fantasy, but it pushes all of the boundaries of those established genres and introduces us to the most memorable characters. This is the beauty of speculative fiction. The ideas are limitless, and in the hands of talented writers we can travel everywhere that can be imagined. The constraints are within the worlds the writer creates and controls, not trapped by the mundane, everyday society and culture of mainstream literature. It truly allows the reader to inhabit different perspectives in new ways.

The several subcategories that emerged with regard to speculative fiction (gay, lesbian, transgender, feminist, black, etc.), enhanced by the different anthologies that we can find in the market, not only signify the portrayal of specific identities or communities, but also each of them seems to address a specific audience. Do you edit and publish with a gendered audience in mind?
I do not. When I think about my audience, I think about what I can bring to them that I know they will love that they don't yet know they will love. In other words, I want to provide them with glorious fiction that they can't get anywhere else. I consider my reading audience to be bright and thoughtful people and willing to go places with me. Also, I am humbled by the many writers who trust me with their stories. It is important to me to introduce those stories to the widest, broadest audience I can.

Of course, not everything will be to everyone's liking. That's fine. But there can still be an appreciation of the work these writers are doing. And I respect the heart and soul that goes into each work of fiction. I also have respect for my reading audience and truly believe that they are longing for more from publishers. My aim is to bring those two worlds together—the writer and the audience. It is my belief that the combination of the two creates something brand new.

In addition, I think about the conversations between the stories when I put together an anthology. How does reading this story *after* reading that one change the experience for the reader? Oftentimes, people will pick up one of my anthologies because they recognize some of the names. And then they can discover all the other writers within the pages. I love it when a reader tells me how excited they were to find a story by XYZ writer that they had never heard of before.

Do you think that speculative fiction and horror stories are differently structured when addressed to traditionally under-portrayed individuals or communities?
I'm not sure what you mean by "differently structured."

In 2015, you published an all-woman, speculative fiction anthology called "Sisters of the Revolution," in which a broad spectrum of genres (horror, science fiction, fantasy, speculative fiction) and identities were represented. What made you think this single-gender format was necessary at the time? Was the mixing of various genres a message to the milieu and the readers?
I am very proud of this anthology, although I can't take complete credit for the idea. My husband was approached by another man who asked him if he'd be willing to select stories for an anthology of this type. He responded by saying he would only do it if I could be his co-editor. It's curious to think that the publisher wasn't considering having a woman be involved from the beginning. Of course, I was very excited to work on this project and put it together. Since Jeff was in the middle of far too many writing deadlines at the time, I did the majority of the work myself.

The anthology was a big hit and I was quite surprised to find how popular it became in Italy. Indeed, Jeff and I were invited to a literary festival in Turin because of this anthology, but sadly Covid-19 came along and dashed those plans.

As with all our anthologies, it was important to show the strength and breadth of this field, which is why I wanted to have stories that had a wide spectrum of ideas and approaches to the subject. I wish the book could have been much larger, but we were constrained by the limits of the publisher. This is why the anthology was presented as the beginning of the conversation. My hope was that there would be additional volumes in an ongoing series, and hopefully this may still happen someday. I would love to see this with new up-and-coming editors from other backgrounds.

You have also published a number of genre-centered anthologies with your husband Jeff VanderMeer. Do you feel that "genre" matters today? What would be its strengths and challenges compared to "high-brow" literature?
This goes back to the earlier discussion of labels. Many of the writers that we've published in our "genre" anthologies are considered "high-brow" writers, but what does that mean, really? Tell a good story and tell it well. That's what really matters. In every project we've undertaken, we aim to push those boundaries as much as possible. We want the reading audience to think about the fiction in new ways.

When we put together *The Weird*, I was thrilled to publish a story by Jamaica Kincaid alongside a story by Stephen King. And why not? Both of the stories fit into the weird category quite well. Tanith Lee and Merce Rodorera—both fabulous storytellers emerging from different backgrounds, languages, and time periods—entice the reader to see the world in mysterious ways. One is considered a genre writer and the other isn't. I find it quite interesting that a lot of fantastical fiction being published outside of the US is considered literary mainstream and yet here we put it in a genre category. (I once jokingly told an American writer friend of mine that if he changed his name to something that sounded Eastern European, the US audiences would consider his work to be more important and not slap a genre label on it.)

I was equally proud to find amazing fiction never published before in English until translated for our anthologies: stories like "The Doom of Principal City" by Russian writer Yefim Zozulya in *The Big Book Of Science Fiction* or "Sowbread" by Sardinian writer Grazia Deledda in *The Big Book Of Classic Fantasy*. Yet, while researching for these projects, I was surprised by how little imagination went into some of the previous anthologies and how limiting they were in their scope. I can't judge too harshly, though, because we had the gift of a much larger word count! And trust me, we took advantage of it, too.

These anthologies have been used often in high schools and universities. I've had the opportunity to make a guest appearance on occasion and it has always been enlightening to engage with the students. Many times, it is their first introduction to "genre" literature and there is always someone who is surprised by a story. When that leads to more discussion on the subject and students seeking additional works by those writers, it makes my heart happy. After all, isn't that what good storytelling is all about?

CHAPTER TWENTY-FOUR

Kaaron Warren

Kaaron Warren (born in 1965) is an award-winning Australian writer of horror, fantasy, and science fiction. Notable works: *Tide of Stone* (novel, 2018), *Into Bones Like Oil* (novella, 2019).

Dear Kaaron Warren, thank you very much for accepting to be part of this volume, which will focus specifically on the notions of "gender" and "genre." Did you or do you feel any gendered resistance in the milieu or in the reviews, specifically in Australia?
I have not personally felt this, but it doesn't mean it doesn't exist. In my opinion, there is more resistance to genre and to small presses rather than gender as far as Australian review spaces goes.

Did you encounter any discrimination specifically related to your gender in your writing career?
Again, not that I was aware of, although I'm certain it occurs.

What is your position on the subject of "genre"? Do you find it problematic or do you accept your writing being categorized in one of these "boxes"?
This is such an interesting and important question. I both find it problematic and accept my writing being categorized! I understand that it is often considered a marketing tool, but I also believe that many readers look for particular themes and ways of telling a story, and genre depictions give them an easy way in. At the library, stickers adorn the books with Crime, Thriller, Romance, Historical, Horror, SF, etc. etc. etc., and this helps the curious reader find new works.

It's problematic only in that it can narrow people's vision. I'm talking about readers as well as mainstream reviewers and curators of writer's festivals, etc. A number of times I've read a piece to a mainstream audience and I've had people tell me, "That's not horror." When I probe further, it's because they liked the story and found it well-written! They connected to characters and, while horrified by events, they understood them. So, they can't see that horror can be well-written, they see it as awful schlock. Hopefully, I am breaking through some of those boundaries, as are the many others writing a "literary" style of horror.

What is determinant in your choice of writing in the horror genre?
These are the stories that present themselves to me; it is the only thing I can truly say. Even if I'm trying to write a nonhorror story, elements will creep in. I was always attracted as a reader to the darker stories. Even in crime fiction, I prefer the stories that have the criminal as a POV (point of view) character rather than the police. I like to know what makes the bad people tick! In my writing, I want to understand why people do what they do, and in horror you can explore this to its very limits. I love the lack of limitation in the genre and the push to go as far as you need to go. There is a painful honesty in the horror genre that you don't always find elsewhere. I think some poetry comes close to the rawness of horror.

What writers have you been influenced by? Was their gender important to you?
Gender was in no way important to me, although many of my influential authors are women.

These writers I consider influential. There are many others who had a small influence! S. E. Hinton, Enid Blyton, Agatha Christie, Ray Bradbury, Harlan Ellison, Daphne du Maurier, Kurt Vonnegut, Celia Fremlin, William Vollman, Edgar Allan Poe, William Golding, Dylan Thomas.

What do you think renders horror genres apt to engage in sexual politics?
The ability to show the monster.

The fact that it can go further than other genres, not restricted by "good taste."

In horror, we can show the truth, the awful reality.

Do you write thinking about a specific audience in mind? Do you think that your reader's gender would impact their reading of your stories?
If I'm writing for a particular market, I will consider the audience. I do think the gender, but perhaps more so the circumstance, of the reader will impact. I know I've had male-identifying readers connect well to stories with a female main character.

Do you think that horror and fantasy works are differently structured when addressed to traditionally under-portrayed individuals or communities?
Not sure, to be honest.

A recurrent theme is your work is infanticide, or situations where children are the victims. Do you feel that this is a specific gendered topic?
This is hard to say. I don't really believe that women write about children more than men.

In many of your stories and novels, especially *Slights*, there is a strong social realist element, which contrasts with many of the settings of the genre. As your protagonists are essentially female, do you see a link in this choice based on the particular class condition of women in Australia?
No, to be honest this was never a consideration. It is social conditions all over, for all genders, sexualities, circumstances, that drive my fiction.

In *Into Bones Like Oil* and *Tide Of Stone*, the supernatural opens up to a possibility of redemption for the female protagonists. Do you think that the horror genre offers more possibilities of identity and situation portrayals for women characters than in the mainstream literary culture?
No, to be honest. I think that in the mainstream, a female character will spend the entire book focusing on identity. In a way, horror is less focused on this because the best of it tells a story at the same time, so that the possibilities of identity and situation are woven into the story rather than being the story itself.

INDEX